# Hands-On Microservices – Monitoring and Testing

A performance engineer's guide to the continuous testing and monitoring of microservices

**Dinesh Rajput**

**BIRMINGHAM - MUMBAI**

# Hands-On Microservices – Monitoring and Testing

**Commissioning Editor:** Richa Tripathi
**Acquisition Editor:** Karan Sadawana
**Content Development Editor:** Mohammed Yusuf Imaratwale
**Technical Editor:** Niral Almeida
**Copy Editor:** Safis Editing
**Project Coordinator:** Hardik Bhinde
**Proofreader:** Safis Editing
**Indexer:** Aishwarya Gangawane
**Graphics:** Jason Monteiro
**Production Coordinator:** Shantanu Zagade

First published: October 2018

Production reference: 2121118

Published by Packt Publishing Ltd.
Livery Place
35 Livery Street
Birmingham
B3 2PB, UK.

ISBN 978-1-78913-360-8

www.packtpub.com

To my country, **India**.

My grandpas, the late **Mr. Arjun Singh** and the late **Mr. Durjan Lal Rajput.**
To all readers of **DineshOnJava** and my books.

To my mother, Indira Devi, and my father, Shrikrashan, for their sacrifices and for
exemplifying the power of determination.

To my kids, Arnav and Rushika, and my wife, Anamika, for being my loving partner
throughout my life journey.

– Dinesh Rajput

`mapt.io`

Mapt is an online digital library that gives you full access to over 5,000 books and videos, as well as industry leading tools to help you plan your personal development and advance your career. For more information, please visit our website.

## Why subscribe?

- Spend less time learning and more time coding with practical eBooks and Videos from over 4,000 industry professionals

- Improve your learning with Skill Plans built especially for you

- Get a free eBook or video every month

- Mapt is fully searchable

- Copy and paste, print, and bookmark content

## Packt.com

Did you know that Packt offers eBook versions of every book published, with PDF and ePub files available? You can upgrade to the eBook version at `www.packt.com` and as a print book customer, you are entitled to a discount on the eBook copy. Get in touch with us at `customercare@packtpub.com` for more details.

At `www.packt.com`, you can also read a collection of free technical articles, sign up for a range of free newsletters, and receive exclusive discounts and offers on Packt books and eBooks.

# Contributors

## About the author

**Dinesh Rajput** is a founder of *Dineshonjava (dot) com*, a blog for Spring and Java techies. He is a Spring enthusiast and a Pivotal Certified Spring Professional. He has written two best-selling books, *Spring 5 Design Patterns* and *Mastering Spring Boot 2.0*. *Mastering Spring Boot 2.0* is the Amazon #1 best-selling book on Java. He has more than 10 years of experience with various aspects of Spring and cloud-native development, such as REST APIs and microservice architecture.

He is currently working as an architect at a leading company. He has worked as a tech lead at Bennett, Coleman & Co. Ltd, and Paytm.

He has a master's degree in computer engineering from JSS Academy of Technical Education, Noida, and lives in Noida with his family.

*Technically, I authored this book, but it was not possible without the unconditional support of my wife. **Anamika** helped me focus on this book. Thanks also to my kids, **Arnav** and **Rushika**. I have taken away a lot of the time that I'd have spent playing with my kids to write this book.*

*Huge thanks go to my father, **Shrikrashan Rajput**, and mother, **Indira Rajput**, and **all my family members**; they always encouraged me to do work that they can feel proud of.*

# About the reviewer

**Mohammad Fahim** has 5 years of experience with Java technology. He did a B.Tech at Punjab Technical University in information technology. He started his career at Innutech Web Sol. Pvt. Ltd. as a software engineer. He is currently working with Sapient Global Markets as a senior associate. He has worked on many projects in sectors such as insurance, education, and production. Fahim is passionate about coding and loves to read articles related to Java technologies. He shares his experience on his blog and writes articles related to Java and web technologies.

> *I would like to thank my family, who always encourage and support me. Also, my friends, who give me strength each day and make my life more meaningful.*

# Packt is searching for authors like you

If you're interested in becoming an author for Packt, please visit `authors.packtpub.com` and apply today. We have worked with thousands of developers and tech professionals, just like you, to help them share their insight with the global tech community. You can make a general application, apply for a specific hot topic that we are recruiting an author for, or submit your own idea.

# Table of Contents

# Preface

*Hands-On Microservices – Monitoring and Testing* is for all software developers and architects who want to learn about using the microservice architecture for enterprise distributed cloud-based applications. The microservice architecture is particularly useful with cloud-native design patterns. Spring Boot 2.0 and Spring Cloud are used with the microservice architecture. The microservice architecture solves the common design problems of the cloud-native infrastructure in distributed applications, and readers will find the examples presented in this book very helpful. We have covered topics from creating microservices to deploying, testing, and monitoring microservices. Before reading this book, readers should have a basic knowledge of design patterns and Spring Boot.

The microservice is not a new concept in software development; it is one of the oldest patterns of software architecture. But nowadays, industries are using this pattern very widely. We can use Spring Boot 2.0 to create microservice-based applications. Spring Boot 2.0 introduces many new features and enhancements to its previous version. We have another book, *Mastering Spring Boot 2.0*, which will give you in-depth insights into Spring Boot and the cloud microservices architecture.

The goals of writing this book are to discuss all the topics related to the microservice architecture and to see how to use this software architecture with cloud-native applications. We have discuss both monolithic and microservices software architectures. We also discuss how to distribute a monolithic application in a microservice-based application, and how to deploy and monitor all microservices.

The book contains nine chapters that cover everything from the development of a microservices-based cloud application to the deployment of microservices either by using virtual machines or container systems such as Docker.

*Hands-On Microservices – Monitoring and Testing* is divided into three parts. The first part introduces you to software architectures, such as monolithic and microservices. Part 2 follows up the explanation of microservices; we will discuss the anatomy of the microservice architecture and microservice deployment patterns. Part 3 expands on that by showing you how to do inter-service communication, and we will discuss various tools and strategies for inter-service communication. Service registry and discovery are other important topics that will be discussed in this book. We will discuss testing and monitoring microservices. Various APM tools are available in the market for monitoring microservices. We will discuss some of these APM tools in this book.

# Who this book is for

*Hands-On Microservices – Monitoring* and Testing is suitable for all software developers and architects. This book is for software professional who wants to learn about the microservice architecture for enterprise distributed cloud-based applications. This book provides in-depth information about the microservice architecture.

# What this book covers

Chapter 1, *Software Architecture Patterns*, explains the concept of conventional monolithic architecture and its advantages in the software development life cycle. It also covers the limitations of the monolithic architecture, which lead to the need to build loosely coupled systems using the microservice architecture.

Chapter 2, *Anatomy of Microservice Decomposition Services*, gives an overview of microservices in detail, explaining the usage of applications and services, the decomposition of the microservice architecture on the basis of business capabilities, and domains and subdomains.

Chapter 3, *Microservices Deployment Patterns*, discusses the deployment of services and communication between these services. You will get an understanding of the microservices deployment structure, approach, and strategies. You will also get a detailed understanding of the flow of microservices, communication, and the various implementation patterns of the microservice architecture.

Chapter 4, *Inter-Service Communication*, looks at how the services within a system communicate with one another.

Chapter 5, *Service Registry and Discovery*, discusses service discovery, explaining how to discover a service in a microservice architecture.

Chapter 6, *External API Gateway*, discusses building microservices using an API gateway. You will get an understanding of how the API gateway helps you to manage APIs and also provides a way for the application's clients to interact with the microservices.

Chapter 7, *Testing of Microservices*, explores various approaches and strategies of testing microservices, microservice test inputs Header, and contains details of the payload. It also discusses the difference between the testing of SOAP and REST services. Popular API testing tools such as Postman, Ready API, JMeter, and Gatling are covered.

Chapter 8, *Performance Testing of Microservices*, explains how to design a strategy to perform performance testing of microservices by studying successful use cases. Furthermore, the chapter demonstrates testing microservices using tools such as JMeter and Loadrunner.

Chapter 9, *Performance Monitoring of Microservices*, discusses how to monitor the performance of microservices. We will discuss various **application performance management (APM)** tools that can be used to test microservices and also discuss performance counters specific to microservices.

# To get the most out of this book

This book can be read without a computer or laptop to hand; you need nothing more than the book itself. However, to follow the examples in the book, you need Java 8, which you can download from http://www.oracle.com/technetwork/java/javase/downloads/jdk8-downloads-2133151.html, and you will also need your favorite IDE for the examples. I have used the **Spring Tool Suite (STS)**. Download the latest version of STS from https://spring.io/tools/sts/all according to your OS. Java 8 and STS work on a variety of platforms, including Windows, macOS, and Linux.

# Download the example code files

You can download the example code files for this book from your account at www.packt.com. If you purchased this book elsewhere, you can visit www.packt.com/support and register to have the files emailed directly to you.

You can download the code files by following these steps:

1. Log in or register at www.packt.com
2. Select the **SUPPORT** tab
3. Click on **Code Downloads & Errata**
4. Enter the name of the book in the **Search** box and follow the onscreen instructions

Once the file is downloaded, please make sure that you unzip or extract the folder using the latest version of:

- WinRAR/7-Zip for Windows
- Zipeg/iZip/UnRarX for Mac
- 7-Zip/PeaZip for Linux

The code bundle for the book is also hosted on GitHub at `https://github.com/PacktPublishing/Hands-On-Microservices-Monitoring-and-Testing`. In case there's an update to the code, it will be updated on the existing GitHub repository.

We also have other code bundles from our rich catalog of books and videos available at `https://github.com/PacktPublishing/`. Check them out!

# Code in action

Visit the following link to check out videos of the code being run:
`http://bit.ly/2Sl3sFJ`

# Conventions used

There are a number of text conventions used throughout this book.

`CodeInText`: Indicates code words in text, database table names, folder names, filenames, file extensions, pathnames, dummy URLs, user input, and Twitter handles. Here is an example: "As you can see, the service name is `account-service`, and it will run on port `1111`."

A block of code is set as follows:

```
<dependency>
          <groupId>org.springframework.boot</groupId>
          <artifactId>spring-boot-starter-test</artifactId>
          <scope>test</scope>
</dependency>
```

When we wish to draw your attention to a particular part of a code block, the relevant lines or items are set in bold:

```
@Service
public class AccountServiceImpl implements AccountService {
@Autowired
          @LoadBalanced
          RestTemplate restTemplate;

          @HystrixCommand(fallbackMethod = "defaultAccount")
          public Account findAccount(Integer accountId) {
                    return
```

```
restTemplate.getForObject("http://ACCOUNT-SERVICE/account/{accountId}",
Account.class, accountId);
        }
```

**Bold**: Indicates a new term, an important word, or words that you see onscreen. For example, words in menus or dialog boxes appear in the text like this. Here is an example: "As you can see in the preceding screenshot, this is done by right-clicking on **Test Plan** and then selecting **Add** | **Threads (Users)** | **Thread Group**."

 Warnings or important notes appear like this.

 Tips and tricks appear like this.

# Get in touch

Feedback from our readers is always welcome.

**General feedback**: If you have questions about any aspect of this book, mention the book title in the subject of your message and email us at customercare@packtpub.com.

**Errata**: Although we have taken every care to ensure the accuracy of our content, mistakes do happen. If you have found a mistake in this book, we would be grateful if you would report this to us. Please visit www.packt.com/submit-errata, selecting your book, clicking on the Errata Submission Form link, and entering the details.

**Piracy**: If you come across any illegal copies of our works in any form on the Internet, we would be grateful if you would provide us with the location address or website name. Please contact us at copyright@packt.com with a link to the material.

**If you are interested in becoming an author**: If there is a topic that you have expertise in and you are interested in either writing or contributing to a book, please visit authors.packtpub.com.

# Reviews

Please leave a review. Once you have read and used this book, why not leave a review on the site that you purchased it from? Potential readers can then see and use your unbiased opinion to make purchase decisions, we at Packt can understand what you think about our products, and our authors can see your feedback on their book. Thank you!

For more information about Packt, please visit `packt.com`.

# Software Architecture Patterns 1

Nowadays, software is not only used for providing services but is also used to develop business. The best-performing software allows a business to grow. Today's application software shouldn't focus on a specific device such as a computer; instead, it should be able to support any platform. As architects, we have to focus on the design of the software application at the time of development. It must be scalable, either vertically or horizontally, and it should be able to cope with millions, or even billions, of requests per second.

In this chapter, we will discuss application architecture patterns, such as the conventional **monolithic architecture pattern** and the **microservice architecture pattern**. We will look at where the concept of conventional monolithic architecture comes from and what advantages it has relating to the software development life cycle. We will also explain the limitations of the monolithic architecture, which leads to the need to build loosely-coupled systems, otherwise known as the **microservice architecture**.

By the end of this chapter, you will be able to understand the traditional approach to building software solutions by adopting a monolithic architecture pattern. You will read about the evolution of the architecture pattern from monolithic to microservice-related. We will also provide a detailed explanation of the microservice architecture and information about how it can be used in this chapter.

This chapter will cover the following topics:

- The monolithic architecture pattern:
  - Example
  - Benefits
  - Limitations
- The microservice architecture pattern:
  - Example
  - Benefits
  - Limitations

- **Service-Oriented Architecture (SOA)**
- SOA versus microservice architecture

Let's get started and look at these topics in detail.

# The monolithic architecture pattern

When I started my job at Paytm, an e-commerce and payment gateway company in India, it was a startup company. We began with monolithic application architecture because there was only two of us there at the time. Many startups begin application development by following monolithic application architecture due to the small size of their team. Monolithic architecture doesn't give you big operational overhead costs, and they often have just one massive codebase.

A monolithic application is a single artifact that includes the interfaces of all layers. For example, a database might have several tables and DAO classes, a client-side UI that includes HTML pages and JavaScript, and a server-side application. This server-side application has to handle HTTP requests, process business logic using service classes, retrieve and update data from the database, exchange messages with other systems, and return responses in an HTML/JSON/XML format. A monolithic application often has a massive codebase which includes all of the aforementioned. As a developer, if you want to make any changes to this massive codebase, you have to build and deploy another updated version of the server-side application.

In a server-side application, you have to focus on development to provide support to a variety of different clients, such as desktop browsers, mobile browsers, and native mobile applications, including Android and iOS. A monolithic application must, therefore, have a complete code in order to support a variety of different clients. Let's discuss an example of a monolithic architecture pattern.

# Monolithic application example

Suppose we are working on an e-commerce application that provides an online bookshop portal. It takes orders from customers, verifies the availability of the ordered book, places an order, and ships the ordered book to the customer. To build this application, we have to create several modules.

These include a Shop Front UI module, which provides a user interface to customers, and backend services, such as an Account Service, a Book Service, an Order Service, a Shipping Service, and so on. These services have various responsibilities, including verifying the customer, checking the availability of books, placing an order, and shipping the order.

All of these modules will be deployed as a single monolithic application either as a WAR file or JAR file. A Java web application as a WAR file runs on a web container such as Tomcat. This web application serves all HTTP requests that come from various clients, such as desktop or mobile browsers. The request comes first to Apache or Nginx and then to Tomcat.

You can also create multiple instances of this monolithic application to handle millions or billions of requests, or include a load balancer to scale and improve availability.

The following diagram illustrates the architectural design of a monolithic application:

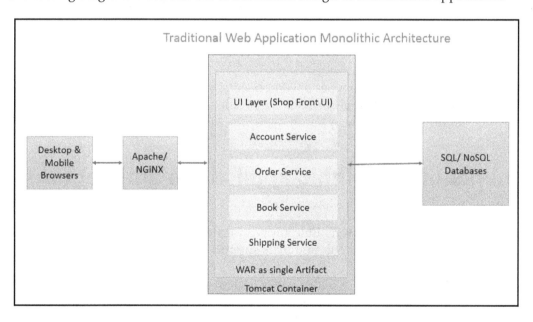

As you can see in the preceding diagram, all modules of this traditional web application, such as **Shop Front UI**, **Account Service**, **Order Service**, **Book Service**, and **Shipping Service**, are single artifacts in the Tomcat container. This monolithic application has a massive codebase that includes all modules. If you introduce new modules to this application, you have to make changes to the existing code and then deploy the artifact with a different code to the Tomcat server.

Server-side application developers can include the following components in the architecture design:

- **Presentation**: This layer handles HTTP requests and responds with HTML, JSON, or XML
- **Business logic**: This is the business logic written into services such as the Account Service or Customer Service
- **Data access**: These objects are responsible for accessing the database for business logic
- **Application integration**: This component is responsible for integrating the application with other external services via messaging or the REST API

In monolithic application architecture, we place such components as a single artifact in the server-side application. This application architecture means that a new team member can be introduced to the application easily due to the close nature of the team. However, when you have to change the application due to scalability or availability requirements, you have to run multiple copies of the application on multiple machines.

Monolithic application architecture can be made logically modular by dividing it into different layers according to the types of components. All modules and different layers are packaged and deployed as a single artifact monolithic application. Let's now move on and look at the benefits of monolithic application architecture.

# Benefits of monolithic application architecture

The monolithic solution has the following benefits:

- **Simple to develop**: Monolithic applications are very simple to develop because current development tools and IDEs support the development of monolithic applications
- **Simple to test**: As we have already discussed, monolithic applications have all of their modules in a single artifact, so you can easily carry out end-to-end testing by simply running the application either manually or with Selenium
- **Simple to deploy**: A monolithic application is a single artifact, so you can easily deploy it to the server as a WAR file
- **Simple to scale**: You can easily achieve scaling by copying the single artifact of the application to multiple running machines and setting up a load balancer behind the monolithic application

As you can see, monolithic applications have numerous benefits. They also have several disadvantages, which we will discuss shortly, but let's first have a look at the situations in which monolithic applications are useful.

# When to use monolithic architecture

Monolithic architecture can be used in the following situations:

- In the foundation stage of projects – most of the time, big, successful applications start with monolithic application architecture
- When building an unproven product or proof of concept
- When your development team is less experienced

Despite the benefits of monolithic application architecture, there are also a few disadvantages.

# Limitations of monolithic application architecture

Monolithic application architecture can sometimes have the following disadvantages:

- A monolithic application has a large codebase, which can intimidate developers, especially those who are new to the team. The application can be difficult to understand and modify. As a result, development is typically quite slow.
- The application is large and complex, which makes it difficult to fully understand and make changes quickly and correctly.
- The impact of a change is usually not very well understood, which leads to carrying out extensive, additional manual testing.
- The architecture can be difficult to scale when different modules have conflicting resource requirements.
- Monolithic applications aren't very reliable; a bug in any module can bring down the whole application.
- They are not very adept at adopting new technologies. Since changes in frameworks or languages will affect an entire application, it is extremely expensive both time-wise and cost-wise.

Let's now discuss which software development processes are better with monolithic architecture.

# Software development processes with monolithic architecture

For a monolithic application, traditional software development processes, such as waterfall processes, are most suitable. This is because a monolithic application usually has large teams working on a single deployment artifact.

As we have discussed, a monolithic application is a single artifact, built as a single unit. This means that it handles the HTTP requests and executes business logic using DAOs to retrieve data from the underlying database at the server-side. However, with a monolithic application, if any changes are made to the application, another version of the entire application will need to be built. Fortunately, this is where the microservice architecture pattern can come to the rescue.

# Microservice architecture pattern

In the previous section, we discussed the monolithic application architecture – in other words, the collection of all modules of an application as a single artifact. There is another architecture pattern that structures an application so that all modules of that application are loosely-coupled, share their services, and are independently deployable. In this approach, each service must be focused on a set of narrowly-related functions and each service runs independently and as a unique process. An application might consist of services, such as the Order Service, the Account Service, and so on. This approach is known as **microservice architecture**.

Microservice architecture refers to a method of software development in which a large software application is divided into several independently deployable services. These services are small, modular, and follow the single responsibility principle of software development. Each service is treated as a unique process that communicates with each other through a well-defined mechanism. We will discuss this further in Chapter 4, *Inter-Service Communication*.

In microservice architecture, all services communicate with each other either synchronously, using HTTP or REST, or asynchronously, using AMQP or Kafka. Each service contains its own database. The basic idea behind microservice architecture is to split up your monolithic application into a set of smaller, interconnected services.

A microservice architecture pattern separates concerns on a process level. All processes in this architecture are loosely coupled with each other. They communicate using predefined rules to achieve a business goal. So, let's move on and look at an example of a microservice-based application.

# Microservice application example

We discussed a monolithic application in the previous section, in the form of an online book shop. In this section, we are going to discuss the same example using microservice architecture. The online bookshop application has four modules; Account Service, Book Inventory Service, Order Service, and Shipping Service. This application also has a user interface application, the Shop Front UI web application, which serves user requests and sends responses.

The following diagram illustrates the architecture of the application, which consists of a set of services:

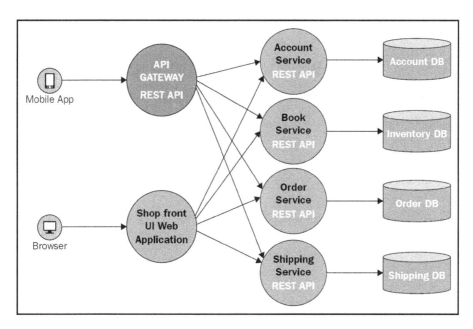

As you can see, we have divided the earlier monolithic bookshop application into several independent services: **Account Service**, **Book Service**, **Order Service**, and **Shipping Service**. This is a microservices architectural style; according to this approach, we can develop a single application as a suite of small services.

Each service is built around a business capability and is independently deployable into the server. For example, the Account Service manages the customer's account and has its own database, Account DB. Similarly, the Book Service manages the inventory of the books and has the database Inventory DB. The Order Service manages the customer's orders using a separate database, Order DB. Finally, the Shipping Service manages shipping orders using the Shipping DB. Each module has its own dependency without depending on other services. This means that we can choose different technologies as well as develop separate services.

The server-side application must handle requests coming from various clients, such as desktop or mobile browsers and native mobile apps. The Shop Front UI web application handles the HTTP requests that come from browsers. Some APIs are exposed to the native mobile app, so the app doesn't call these APIs directly – instead, the app communicates through an intermediary known as an API Gateway. The API Gateway is responsible for handling these requests using load balancing. The API Gateway also offers caching, access control, and API monitoring.

We'll discuss the benefits of the microservice architecture pattern in the following section.

# Benefits of microservice application architecture

The following are some of the benefits of the microservice architecture pattern:

- **Easy to maintain**: It is very easy for the developer to understand; this way, you can start development faster, which in turn makes it more productive
- **Easy to scale**: You can easily scale individual components
- **Technology diversity**: Microservices allow you to mix libraries, frameworks, data storage, and languages
- **Fault isolation**: Component failure should not bring the whole system down
- **Better support**: The architecture is suitable for smaller, parallel teams
- **Independent deployment**: We can easily deploy each microservice independently without impacting other microservices in the architecture

Microservice-based architecture also has a few disadvantages, however, and we'll take a look at them in the following section.

# Disadvantages of the microservice architecture pattern

Microservices provide several benefits, but there are also some challenges relating to microservice architecture when developing an enterprise application. These include the following:

- It is sometimes difficult to achieve strong consistency across services and transactions.
    - **Atomicity**, **Consistency**, **Isolation**, **Durability** (**ACID**) transactions do not span multiple processes. ACID is a set of properties of database transactions intended to guarantee validity, even in the event of errors, power failures, and so on. This can be counteracted, however, using eventual consistency, which helps to manage transactions in a microservice application.
- A distributed system often:
    - Is harder to debug or trace
    - Has a greater need for end-to-end testing
    - Requires you to expect, test for, and handle the failure of any process
    - Has more components to maintain, which leads to issues such as redundancy or **High Availability** (**HA**)
- It typically requires a *cultural* change with regards to DevOps, such as how applications are developed and deployed, and the cooperation of Development and Operation teams

In light of its disadvantages, in the next section, we will discuss when to use microservice architecture for your project.

# When to use microservice architecture

One of the challenges related to microservice architecture is deciding when to use it. The following scenarios are examples of when it is a good idea to start using microservice architecture in your project:

- **New project development**: Microservice architecture is more suitable when developing the first version of an application. You can plan your project and its associated modules from an initial level, whereas it can be challenging to convert an old or legacy project into a microservice-based application.

- **Separating concerns in the business application**: This architecture provides a better level of separation of concerns as the Spring framework provides separation of concerns at the level of the application's components.
- **Development of a cloud-native application**: This architecture provides cloud-native patterns and supports distributed application development. We can create numerous independent services which can be deployed to a different platform on a different network, as can be done in the cloud.
- **Quick development of independent service delivery**: Microservice architecture allows us to develop a business application quickly by dividing it into the independent delivery of individual parts within a larger, integrated system.
- **Efficient modules**: In a business application, there are some modules that are very important for a business, and these modules must be developed in extremely efficient ways. Microservice architecture allows you to use better technologies for these modules to improve their efficiency.
- **Alongside a fast-growing product or team**: If you start with microservice architecture, it provides your team with the flexibility to develop a product quickly. It also provides scalability to your application from the beginning.

Essentially, microservice-based application development better follows an agile software development process, because different, small teams work on separate modules of the application. The teams are therefore able to release services with continuous delivery. Now, let's move on to another type of software application architecture.

# Service-oriented architecture (SOA)

SOA is another application architectural style. In SOA, architecture services are provided to other services and to vendor components using a communication protocol over a network. These services are discrete units of functionalities that can be accessed remotely. The following diagram shows an SOA in action:

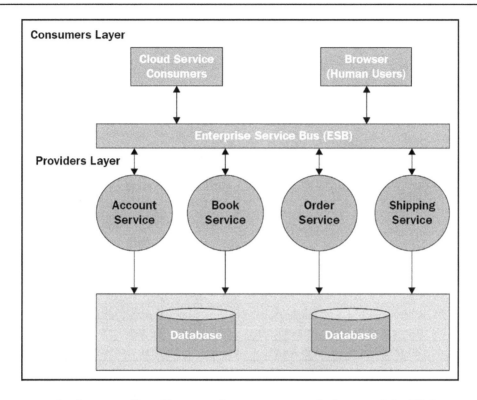

As you can see in the preceding diagram, there are two main layers of the SOA: a **service consumer layer** and a **service provider layer**. The service consumer layer is the point at which all the consumers, such as human consumers and other service consumers, interact with the SOA. The provider layer is the point where all services are defined within the SOA.

In the preceding diagram, the **Enterprise Service Bus** (**ESB**) provides communication by a common communication protocol, or communication bus, which has connections between the consumers and providers. In SOA architecture, database storage is shared between all services.

SOA has more dependent ESBs. The ESBs implement a communication system between mutually interacting software applications with microservices. It also uses faster messaging mechanisms.

Let's now move on and take a look at the differences between SOA and microservice architecture.

# SOA versus microservice architecture

The following table lists some of the differences between SOA and microservice architecture:

| Service-oriented Architecture (SOA) | Microservice architecture |
|---|---|
| Focuses on imperative programming | Focuses on a responsive actor programming style |
| Its models tend to have an outsized relational database | Microservices frequently use NoSQL or micro-SQL databases (which can be connected to conventional databases) |
| In SOA, ESB implements communication between mutually-interacting software | In microservices, independent processes communicate with each other using language-agnostic APIs |
| It is easier to deploy new versions of services frequently, or scale a service independently | Services can operate and be deployed independently of other services |
| SOA has ESB, which could be a single point of failure that impacts the entire application | Microservice architecture has a much better fault-tolerance system |
| Data storage is shared between services | Each service has its own data storage |

# Summary

In this chapter, we discussed different software application architecture patterns, including monolithic, microservice, and SOAs. Monolithic architecture means building an application that includes all of its modules as a single artifact. It is better for simple and lightweight applications,

but it has various drawbacks, such as its large codebase, which can become difficult to manage. Even after making only a small change to the codebase, a new version of the complete application codebase must be built and deployed to the server. To resolve the problems of monolithic architecture, microservice architecture can be used.

Microservice-based architecture resolves many of the problems of monolithic architecture. This architecture pattern decomposes a monolithic application into several different and independent processes. These processes are known as **microservices**. A microservice architecture pattern is the better choice for complex, evolving applications. In essence, this architecture pattern handles a complex system better than monolithic architecture.

In Chapter 2, *Anatomy of Microservice Decomposition Services*, we'll look at how to decompose services in microservice architecture.

# 2
# Anatomy of Microservice Decomposition Services

In Chapter 1, *Software Architecture Patterns*, we discussed the microservice architecture and its benefits and challenges. The microservice architecture approach is all about dividing a complex monolithic application into several different independent services, which run independently on several machines or cloud servers. In this chapter, we will discuss the anatomy of the microservice architecture and look at how to decompose a monolithic application into a number of processes.

This chapter will discuss microservices in detail, including how to use applications and services. We will also look at the decomposition of the microservice architecture on the basis of business capability and the domain and subdomain.

By the end of this chapter, you will understand how microservices are built and will be able to build your own. You will also learn why the microservice architecture is loosely coupled and the difference between **Simple Object Access Protocol (SOAP)** and **RESTful microservices**.

This chapter will cover the following topics:

- Anatomy of a microservice
- Decomposition based on business capability
- Decomposition based on domain
- Microservice chassis for common cross-cutting concerns
- Building microservices
- SOAP versus RESTful microservices

Let's look at these topics in detail.

# Anatomy of a microservice

One of the biggest challenges in using a microservice architecture is deciding how to break an existing, complex monolithic system into several services. A microservice architecture structures a complex system into more manageable, separate services, each of which focuses on a specific part of your business goal.

As we know, managing complex monolithic applications is much harder than managing a small service, for developers as well as **Quality Assurance** (**QA**) teams. A potential method of reducing the complexity of a monolithic application is by using a distributed application development approach, which refers to the decomposition of a monolithic application into several smaller microservices. It is important to consider how microservices can be made to achieve the same business goal as the original monolithic application. Microservices provide a perfect modularity due to their independent design, development, deployment, and maintenance. Let's look at the following monolithic application diagram:

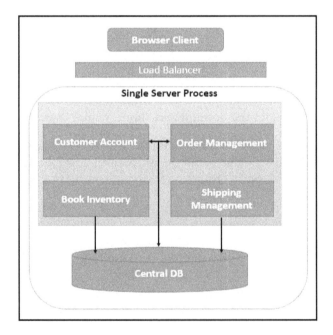

As you can see, the application is packaged as a single WAR or EAR file. All the services related to this application run in the single-server process. It uses the central database and is based on a centralized services approach.

Let's move on to looking at how to decompose this application into microservices. One of the challenges of decomposing a monolithic application is deciding into which modules it should be divided. This depends on your business application and how many modules you want to create.

# Context boundaries

A module is just a way of defining a context boundary. If you want to migrate your existing monolithic application to a microservice-based application, you first have to identify a hidden context within your current application. This means we have to define the context and draw explicit context boundaries. This helps us design a robust microservice-based application.

For example, a typical online book shopping portal can have an order and shipping module using the same entity product. The following diagram shows the context boundaries of this application:

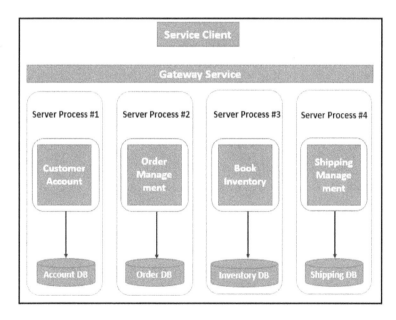

As you can see in the preceding diagram, the distributed application is based on different bounded contexts. The preceding design is a modular application design, where every module runs an independent process as a service. This is a decentralized approach to application design.

Once you have defined context boundaries, you can then easily decompose your existing monolithic application into a microservice-based application, where each bounded context has one microservice. In the example shown in the previous diagram, we have divided our monolithic application into four bounded contexts, which means that there are four microservices: Order Service, Book Service, Shipping Service, and Customer Service.

We now have a separate product entity in the Order Service and the Shipping Service, which each have their respective repositories. This concept can be extended by defining explicit context boundaries for the Stock and Inventory modules and creating an independent microservice for each.

Let's have a look at two different decomposition approaches. A monolithic application can be decomposed based on either its business capability or its domain.

# Decomposition based on business capability

Business capability refers to structured modeling, which provides a high-level overview of the business. Business capabilities are the top layer of the business architecture and belong to the business domain. We can split a monolithic application into services based on their business capabilities. These services have broad context boundaries, including user interface, persistent storage, and any external collaborations. Consequently, the teams are cross-functional and include the full range of skills required for the development: user experience, database, and project management.

A business capability refers to how a business architecture model behaves in order to achieve a business goal. A business capability is similar to a business object. Let's define the services of our application based on its business capabilities:

- **Customer Account Management** is responsible for managing the account details of the customers
- **Order Management** is responsible for managing the customer's orders
- **Book Inventory Management** is responsible for managing the book inventories
- **Shipping Management** is responsible for managing shipped orders

It is important to understand the core components of the business, such as the user interface, service, data, logging, or messaging. Business capabilities mostly depend on the business and are primarily organized in multiple layers.

A microservice architecture would have services that correspond to each of these capabilities, as follows:

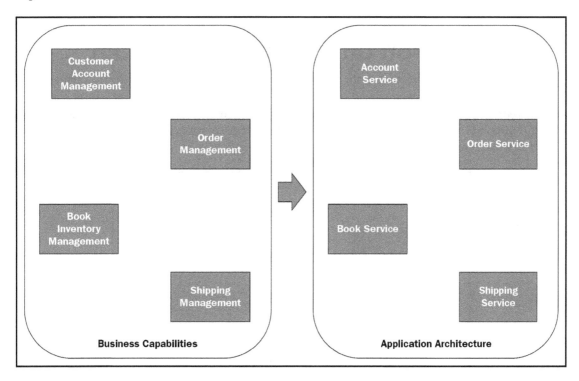

The preceding diagram shows the decomposition of a monolithic application based on its business capabilities. We have identified four business capabilities of the online bookshop application and created a service to correspond to each.

The challenging part of this decomposition is how to identify the business capabilities. Nobody identifies business capabilities perfectly, but a useful place to start is by analyzing the organization's purpose, structure, and business processes. This approach has the following benefits:

- The architecture is stable since the business capabilities are relatively stable.
- In the microservice architecture, each development team focuses on delivering business value rather than technical features. These teams are cross-functional and autonomous.
- The microservice approach provides a cohesive system that has loosely coupled services.

Let's move on to the next section, where we will discuss another approach for decomposing a monolithic application to a microservice-based application.

# Decomposition on the basis of domain

You can also split a monolithic application into a microservice-based application based on its domain. The domain decomposition methods focus on a bounded context, which is a central pattern of **Domain-Driven Design** (**DDD**). Domain decomposition methods split a domain into subdomains. You can define services that correspond to the subdomains of the DDD, as shown in the following diagram:

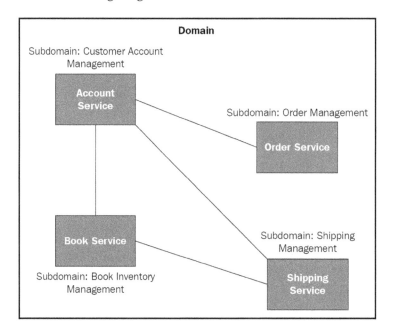

The preceding diagram shows a decomposition based on subdomains. Each subdomain has a corresponding service. Subdomains can be classified according to business processes. For example, as you can see in the preceding diagram, we have decomposed the online bookshop application into the following subdomains:

- **Customer Account Management**
- **Book Inventory Management**
- **Order Management**
- **Shipping Management**

The main challenge of this approach lies in identifying the subdomains. Like business capabilities, subdomains are identified by analyzing the business and its organizational structure and identifying the different areas of expertise. Let's discuss the microservice chassis for common cross-cutting concerns.

# Microservice chassis to handle cross-cutting concerns

In any new application development, you are often required to implement particular scenarios or services, such as cross-cutting concerns. You have to spend a significant amount of time implementing common cross-cutting concerns in the development of a new application. Let's have a look at the following cross-cutting concerns:

- **Build system and externalized configuration**: We have to choose either a Maven or a Gradle-based system to compile, package, version, and resolve external dependencies. This will also deal with further external configurations, such as credentials, and the network locations of external services, including databases or message brokers.
- **Implement logging**: Logging is also required for all services of a new application development. You have to configure a logging framework, such as Java, Log4j, Logj42, `java.util.logging`, Commons Logging, Logback, or slf4j.
- **Monitoring and health checks**: You have to implement a monitoring system for all services in a new application development. Spring Boot applications are very easy to monitor using the Spring Boot Actuator and JMX. You have to provide a URL for the health check of the application.
- **Metrics**: The Spring Boot Actuator also provides the metrics of an application. Metrics provide an insight into what the application is doing and how it is performing.
- **Distributed tracing**: A microservice architecture is based on distributed services across a number of machines, so it needs to be able to trace a complete call end to end across multiple services. Spring Cloud provides a solution for distributed tracing using Spring Cloud Sleuth and Zipkin. It assigns each external request to a unique identifier, which is passed across the services to trace a complete task.

The preceding list shows the most common cross-cutting concerns. There are many others which are specific to each technology. Suppose you want to configure a database and a message broker in a distributed application. You have to handle the external configuration and the boilerplate code across the services in the distributed application so that the relational database is configured with a connection pool. In order to implement these common concerns, we have to write repetitive code. According to the programming principle of **Don't Repeat Yourself (DRY)**, we must avoid code repetition in any of our application infrastructures.

A microservice chassis provides a way of implementing these cross-cutting concerns without repeating the same code across multiple services in the distributed programming model. We can build a reusable chassis and use it across services by asking teams to ensure that the search service shares the same coding pattern. We can create a production-ready chassis, using Spring Boot and Spring Cloud, that you can use to bootstrap your own cloud applications.

For more information, please refer to my book *Mastering Spring Boot 2.0*, which has some examples of these cross-cutting concerns. In *Mastering Spring Boot 2.0*, I used the following frameworks and components for the microservice chassis:

- **Runtime monitoring**: Spring Boot Actuator, Spring Boot Admin, and JMX
- **Service registration and discovery**: Spring Cloud Netflix (Eureka)
- **Distributed call tracing**: Spring Cloud Sleuth and Zipkin
- **Logging**: Slf4j and Logback
- **Optional runtime container**: Docker and AWS ECS

Let's continue with our online bookshop example and look at how to build microservices using Spring Boot and Spring Cloud.

# Building microservices

In this section, we will discuss how to build a microservice-based application using the same online bookshop example as in the previous sections. Our application has the following four modules:

- **Customer Account Management**
- **Order Management**
- **Book Inventory Management**
- **Shipping Management**

I will create a microservice for each of these modules. The following microservices correspond to the application modules:

- Customer Account Management → Account Service
- Order Management → Order Service
- Book Inventory Management → Book Service
- Shipping Management → Shipping Service

The following diagram shows the architecture of this online bookshop application:

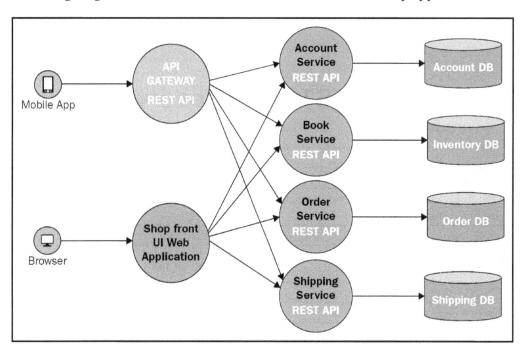

As you can see in the preceding diagram, we have four core microservices in this application. This architecture also has two more services: an API Gateway and the Shopfront UI web application, which is the user interface that can be seen on the browser. To start building our microservice project, we have to create the following individual services:

- Config Server
- Eureka Server
- Account Service

- Book Service
- Order Service
- Shipping Service
- Zuul Proxy API Gateway

I have implemented these services using Spring Boot and Spring Cloud. You can use `http://start.spring.io/` to generate the Spring Boot project. In this book, I haven't included the complete code structure for this application, but you can find it on GitHub: `https://github.com/PacktPublishing/Mastering-Spring-Boot-2.0`.

We'll look at the difference between SOAP and RESTful microservices in the following section.

# SOAP versus RESTful microservices

SOAP and RESTful microservices have the following differences:

| SOAP | RESTful microservices |
|---|---|
| An XML-based message protocol. | An architectural style. |
| Uses WSDL for communication between the consumer and the provider. | Use XML or JSON to send and receive data. |
| Invokes services by calling the RPC method. | Simply call services via the URL path. |
| The transfer is over HTTP. Also uses other protocols, such as SMTP or FTP. | The transfer is over HTTP only. |
| SOAP-based reads can't be cached. | RESTful microservice reads can be cached. |
| SOAP is not very scalable | RESTful microservices are very scalable. |
| SOAP is more suitable for enterprise systems and high-security systems, such as a banking system. | RESTful microservices are suitable for all types of systems apart from where high security and high reliability is critical. |
| Doesn't support error handling | Has built-in error handling. |
| Uses service interfaces to expose the business logic. | Uses URI to expose business logic. |

# Summary

In this chapter, we have discussed the decomposition of a monolithic application into a microservice-based architecture. You can decompose a monolithic application based on either its business capabilities or its domain. Business capabilities are the processes that are required for the business goal. In domain-based decomposition, we can use a bounded context, which is a central pattern for the DDD. In the DDD, we have to identify the domain's subdomains, each of which has a corresponding service in the application architecture.

We have built an online bookshop application with a microservice architecture. We have also discussed the differences between SOAP and RESTful microservices.

In `Chapter 3`, *Microservices Deployment Patterns*, we'll gain an understanding of how to deploy microservices and how these services communicate with each other in the architecture.

# 3
# Microservices Deployment Patterns

In the previous chapters, we discussed the evolution of the microservice architecture and how it can be thought of as a set of services. We have also discussed the deployment and packaging of these services. This chapter will explore various microservices deployment patterns and look at how to deploy microservices so that they can be easily scaled to handle a large number of requests from other integrated components.

In this chapter, the reader will learn about the deployment of services. You will get an understanding of the structure, approach, and strategy of microservices deployment. We will also look in detail at the flow of microservices with various implementation patterns.

This chapter will cover the following topics:

- Microservices deployment patterns:
  - Multiple instances of microservices per host
  - A single instance of a microservice per host
  - A single instance of a microservice per VM
  - A single instance of a microservice per container
- Microservices deployment platforms
- Serverless deployment

Let's have a look at these topics in detail.

# Microservices deployment

In Chapter 2, *Anatomy of Microservice Decomposition Services*, we created a distributed application based on the microservice architecture and architected the application as a set of services. We can now deploy each service as a set of service instances to improve throughput and availability. The microservice architecture makes the service deployable and scalable, meaning all service instances are isolated from each other.

The microservice architecture allows us to build and deploy a service quickly. It also allows us to limit the number of resources used, including CPU, memory, and I/O resources. A microservice application has tens of hundreds of services. You can independently increase or decrease resources of a deployment machine based on the usage of a service. Microservices also allow you to write a service in any language and framework, so you can provide the infrastructure for a service accordingly. You can monitor each service independently and deploy a service according to its behavior.

For example, imagine that you need to run a service with a certain number of instances based on the demand for the service in a business application. With a microservice application, you can easily achieve this by adding multiple VMs or containers for that particular service. You can also provide the appropriate CPU, memory, and I/O resources for each instance. The challenging aspect of a microservice application is that the service deployment must be fast, reliable, and cost-effective.

We have a few strategies that we can use to deploy the microservices of a distributed application; they are as follows:

- Multiple instances of microservices per host
- A single instance of a microservice per host:
    - A single instance of a microservice per VM
    - A single instance of a microservice per container

These microservice deployment patterns were suggested by Chris Richardson on his blog, https://microservices.io/.

Let's now have a look at each strategy in detail.

# Multiple instances of microservices per host

According to this strategy, multiple instances of a microservice run on one or more physical or virtual hosts. In this approach, each instance of the service runs on a different, well-known port on one or more virtual or physical machines. This is a very traditional approach to microservice application deployment and is illustrated in the following diagram:

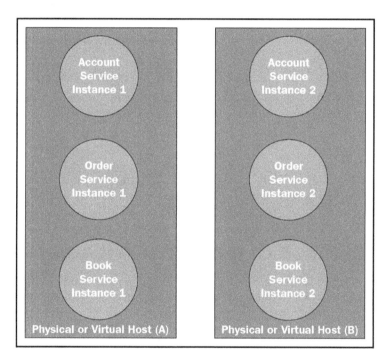

The preceding diagram shows the structure of this pattern. There are two physical or virtual hosts (A and B). These hosts have multiple instances of microservices for our application, and they are **Account Service**, **Order Service**, and **Book Service**.

You can achieve this pattern of microservice deployment using the following methods:

- Deploying multiple instances of microservices on the same Apache Tomcat server or in the same JVM
- Deploying an instance of a microservice as a JVM process or on an Apache Tomcat server, such as a Tomcat instance, per service instance

This pattern has the following benefits:

- It has more efficient resource utilization than other approaches
- Deploying a service instance is relatively fast

However, this approach also has the following disadvantages:

- There is no isolation between the instances of microservices; therefore, a defective service instance could produce noise or affect other services in the same process
- It could create conflict over resource utilization between instances of microservices
- It could also cause problems due to a conflict between versions
- We can't assign a specific amount of resource utilization, nor can we increase the resource capacity for a specific instance of microservices
- It is also difficult to monitor resource utilization independently for one instance of a microservice

As mentioned earlier, this is the traditional approach to deploying microservices, so it has more limitations than the others. Let's now move on to some other approaches.

# A single instance of a microservice per host

According to this approach, we deploy a single instance of a microservice on its own single host. A service instance is deployed to its own host and each service instance runs independently. This approach has two specific patterns:

- A single instance of a microservice per VM
- A single instance of a microservice per container

A host can be a physical machine, a virtual machine, or a container such as a **Docker container**. The following diagram demonstrates this approach of deploying microservices:

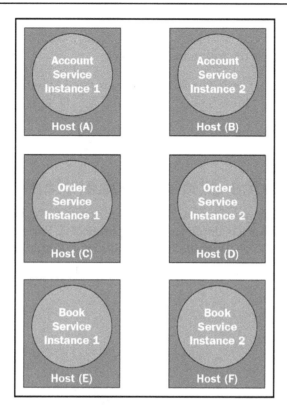

As you can see in the preceding diagram, there is a number of hosts, each of which holds several instances of services. Each service instance has been deployed on its own host machine, that is either a VM or a container. Let's now discuss the benefits and drawbacks of this approach.

# Benefits

This approach has the following benefits:

- It provides complete isolation between instances of microservices
- We can easily correct a defective service without affecting other services
- There is no resource utilization conflict between instances of microservices because each service runs on a separate host using its own resources; in other words, there are no resources shared between instances of microservices
- We can assign a specific amount of resources to a microservice instance on demand
- We can easily monitor, manage, and redeploy each service instance

## Drawbacks

However, this approach has the following drawback:

- It has less efficient resource utilization compared to with multiple instances of microservices per host

Let's have a look at the two different types of this pattern.

# A single instance of a microservice per VM

According to this approach, you can package the service as a VM image and use this to deploy it. The service instance is deployed as a separate VM. For example, we can use an AWS EC2 instance as a VM, as illustrated in the following diagram:

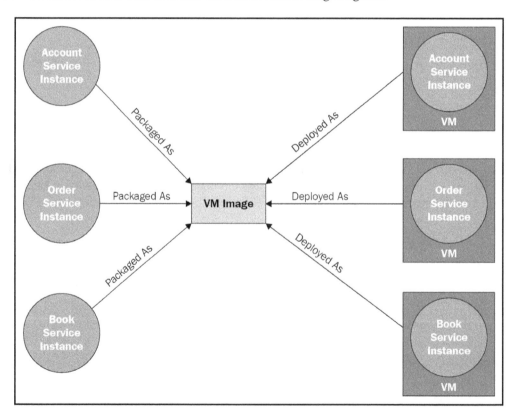

As you can see in the preceding diagram, this pattern packages an instance of the service as a VM image and launches the VM images as a running process, such as the Amazon EC2 AMI.

Many companies use this approach to deploy microservices, such as Netflix, who use this pattern to deploy their video streaming service. Netflix packages an instance of the video streaming service as an EC2 AMI using Aminator, with each instance running as an EC2 instance. Other companies who use this pattern include Boxfuse and Cloud Native.

There are various tools available on the market to package instances of your services as VM images. For example, Jenkins invokes Aminator to build an instance of your service as an EC2 AMI. Similarly, Packer creates VM images through multiple virtualization technologies such as EC2, DigitalOcean, VirtualBox, and VMware.

Let's now move on and have a look at the benefits and drawbacks of this approach.

# Benefits

This approach has the following benefits:

- It is easy to scale by increasing the number of instances; if you use this pattern, you can use the power of the mature cloud infrastructure. For example, AWS provides auto-scaling groups to scale the service automatically based on the traffic or load to the service. AWS also provides another useful feature, which is the Elastic Load Balancer.
- It is very isolated, which means that each service instance runs independently without being hampered by other services.
- Each instance has a fixed amount of resources, such as CPU or memory, and no other service can share its resources.
- Deployment is much simpler and more reliable.
- A VM encapsulates your services, along with the required technologies inside a virtual box, similar to a black box.

# Drawbacks

However, this pattern does have the following disadvantages:

- Resource utilization is less efficient
- Building a VM image is time-consuming

- It requires you to build and manage VMs – although there are some tools such as Boxfuse that provide a solution for this

Let's have a look at another, more lightweight approach to deploying microservices: the *single instance of microservices per container* pattern.

# A single instance of microservice per container

According to this approach, each instance of a microservice runs on its own individual lightweight container. The container is nothing but a virtualization mechanism at the operating system level. This means that you can package your service as a container image, such as a Docker image, and you can deploy that image as a container, as illustrated in the following diagram:

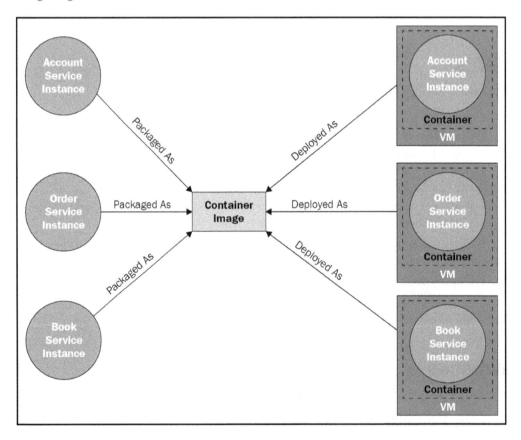

As you can see in the preceding diagram, each container is virtualized over the operating system of the VM.

Docker is one of the most popular container-based technologies. Docker provides a way of packaging and deploying services. Each service is packaged as a Docker image, which is then deployed as a Docker container. You can use Docker containers with the following Docker clustering frameworks to manage your containers:

- Kubernetes
- Marathon/Mesos
- Amazon EC2 Container Service

Docker images have their own port namespace and root filesystem and you can also set a resource utilization limit for each container.

Let's have a look at the benefits and drawbacks of this method.

# Benefits

The benefits of the container approach are similar to those of the VM approach. It also has the following additional advantages:

- Unlike VMs, containers are a lightweight technology
- Building a container image is much faster than building a VM image; this is because the container doesn't have any lengthy OS boot mechanisms and it starts only the application process, rather than an entire OS
- Each service instance is isolated, just like the VM approach

# Drawbacks

This pattern has the following drawbacks:

- Currently, the container infrastructure is not as mature as the infrastructure for VMs
- The container infrastructure is not secure as the infrastructure for VMs
- Containers don't provide as rich an infrastructure as VMs
- It has less efficient resource utilization compared to the multiple services per host pattern because there are more hosts

We've now looked at multiple different approaches to deploying microservices. You can choose either VMs or containers for deploying microservices, according to your requirements.

Another method of deploying microservices that is becoming increasingly popular is serverless deployment. In the next section, we'll learn how to deploy microservices in a serverless environment.

# Service deployment platforms

There are several deployment platforms available that provide automated infrastructure for application deployment. These provide a lot of services that can be used for service deployment, such as load balancing. These platforms include the following:

- Container-based deployment platforms, such as Docker orchestration frameworks, including Docker Swarm mode and Kubernetes
- Serverless platforms, such as AWS Lambda
- Cloud-based platforms, such as PaaS, including CloudFoundry, and AWS Elastic Beanstalk

Internally, deployment platforms are also used with either a VM or containers to deploy microservices. We looked at how Dockers and AWS platforms can be used to deploy microservices in our previous book, *Mastering Spring Boot 2.0*.

So, let's now move on and discuss serverless deployment.

# Serverless deployment

If you want to avoid choosing between using VMs or a container, you can opt for a serverless microservice deployment instead. Serverless deployment is a cloud-based deployment model in which the cloud provider manages all resources that are utilized by microservices dynamically. They charge based on the actual usage of resources by microservices.

Serverless cloud computing is provided by cloud vendors such as Amazon, Google, or Microsoft. Amazon provides AWS Lambda as a serverless deployment technology, which supports Java, Python, and Node.js languages. You can easily deploy microservices to the serverless platform by packaging the microservices as ZIP files and uploading them to AWS Lambda. The serverless platform automatically runs instances of your microservices to handle incoming requests. Serverless cloud computing also uses resources such as the server, memory, and CPU, but you don't have to worry about the infrastructure.

Google provides the Google Cloud Function as a **Function as a Service** (**FaaS**), and Microsoft provides the Azure Function. Amazon's AWS Lambda function is a stateless service.

# Summary

In this chapter, we have learned about the deployment patterns of microservices. We have discussed various deployment strategies, including the multiple instances of microservices per host pattern, the single instance of a microservice per host pattern, the single instance of a microservice per VM pattern, and the single instance of a microservice per container pattern. This gave you an understanding of the different structures, approaches, and strategies used when deploying microservices.

We have also seen how to deploy microservices using a serverless infrastructure such as AWS Lambda, or the Azure Function to resolve the issue of having to choose between using VMs and containers.

In Chapter 4, *Inter-Service Communication*, we'll gain an understanding of how services communicate with each other in the microservice architecture.

# 4
# Inter-Service Communication

In Chapter 1, *Software Architecture Patterns*, we learned about monolithic and microservice-based architectures and discussed their benefits and drawbacks. In Chapter 2, *Anatomy of Microservice Decomposition Services*, we looked at the various ways of decomposing a monolithic application into a microservice-based application, and we also built an application based on a microservice architecture. In chapter 3, *Microservices Deployment Patterns*, we discussed various strategies for deploying microservice-based applications. In this chapter, we will take a look at how the services within a system communicate with one another.

In a monolithic application, there is no need for inter-service communication or internal business functionality. The components invoke other components by calling a language-level method or through a simple function call. However, in the case of a microservice-based application, the components might not be part of the same service or machine. Instead, they might run on several machines or different clouds. Each service is typically a process, so you have to call other processes or services using various patterns to provide communication over different networks.

In this chapter, we will cover various inter-service communication strategies for either synchronous communication or asynchronous communication. We will also discuss **Remote Procedure Invocations (RPIs)**, such as REST, gRPC, and Apache Thrift.

This chapter will cover the following topics:

- Approaches to service communication:
    - Synchronous communication
    - Asynchronous communication
- Messaging
- Transactional messaging
- Event-based communication
- Microservice implementation patterns:
    - The **Command Query Responsibility Segregation pattern (CQRS)**
    - The Event Sourcing pattern
    - The Eventual Consistency pattern
- Domain-specific protocols

Let's get started and have a look at these topics in detail.

# Approaches to service communication

In the microservice architecture pattern, a distributed system runs on several different machines, and each service is a component or process of an enterprise application. The services in these multiple machines must handle requests from the clients of the enterprise application. Sometimes, all of the services involved collaborate to handle such requests; the services interact using an inter-service communication mechanism.

However, in the case of a monolithic application, all components are part of the same application and run on the same machine. This means that the monolithic application doesn't require an inter-service communication mechanism. Have a look at the following diagram, which uses the Bookshop application from before and compares the two communication methods:

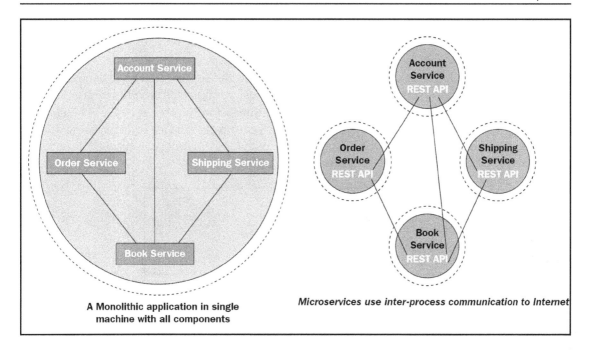

A Monolithic application in single
machine with all components

*Microservices use inter-process communication to Internet*

As you can see in the preceding diagram, a monolithic application has all of its components combined as a single artifact and deployed to a single machine. One component calls another using language-level method calls. However, in the microservice architecture, all components of the application run on multiple machines as a process or service and they use inter-process communication to interact with each other.

In the microservice architecture, there are two approaches to inter-process communication, which are as follows:

- The synchronous communication style
- The asynchronous communication style

Let's have a look at these communication styles in detail.

# Synchronous communication

In this communication style, the client service expects a response within a period of time. It blocks the thread while it is waiting for a response from the server. This style can be used with HTTP protocols – usually REST. This is the easiest possible solution for inter-service communication. The client can make a REST call to interact with other services. The client sends a request to the server and waits for a response from the service (mostly using a JSON response over HTTP). Spring Cloud Netflix provides the most common pattern for synchronous REST communication such as **Feign** or **Hystrix**.

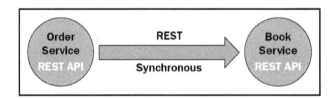

In the preceding diagram, the Order Service calls the Book Service and waits for the response to be returned. The Order Service can then process the Book Service's response in the same transaction that triggered the communication.

The synchronous communication approach does have some drawbacks, such as **timeouts** and **strong coupling**. For example, the Order Service needs to wait for the response from the Book Service, and the strong coupling means that the Order Service can't work without the Book Service being available. We can avoid this coupling by using the Hystrix library, which enables us to use fallbacks in case the service is not available at that time.

There are numerous protocols, such as **REST**, **gRPC**, and **Apache Thrift**, that can be used to interact with services synchronously.

# REST

REST is an architectural style that describes best practices for exposing web services over HTTP. **REpresentational State Transfer** (**REST**), was coined by **Roy Fielding**. It is based on HTTP as an application protocol. REST is not just a means of transport, a framework, or specification, but instead is a style that emphasizes scalability.

Nowadays, RESTful is a popular style for developing APIs for enterprise application. REST is an architecture style and is used in the **Inter-Process Communication** (**IPC**) mechanism that uses HTTP. A resource is a key concept in REST architecture. It represents a business object such as an account or a customer; it can also represent a collection of business objects. In REST style, HTTP verbs are used as the actions for manipulating resources, and these actions are referenced using a URL.

REST services expose resources through URIs, such as the following: `https://www.dineshonjava.com/book-shop/books/123456789`. Resources support a limited set of operations such as `GET`, `PUT`, `POST`, and `DELETE` in the case of HTTP. All of these have well-defined semantics. For example, we can update the order `PUT` by calling `/orders/123`, but we can't update `POST` using `/order/edit?id=123`.

In REST services, clients can request a particular representation. Resources can support multiple representations, such as HTML, XML, or JSON, and representations of a resource can link to other resources. When using **Hypermedia As The Engine of Application State** (**HATEOAS**), the RESTful responses contain the links you need, just like HTML pages do.

RESTful services use a stateless architecture, so there is no HttpSession usage. The `GET` operations can be cached on URLs. REST provides looser coupling between the client and the server. HTTP headers and status codes communicate the result to clients.

> *REST provides a set of architectural constraints that, when applied as a whole, emphasize the scalability of component interactions, the generality of interfaces, independent deployment of components, and intermediary components to reduce interaction latency, enforce security, and encapsulate legacy systems.*
>
> *– Roy Fielding, Architectural Styles and the Design of Network-based Software Architectures.*

Let's have a look at the following diagram, which explains what a synchronous REST call is:

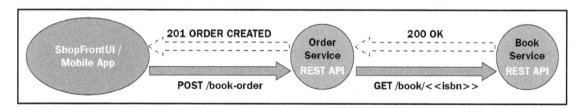

In the preceding diagram, the **ShopFrontUI** web or mobile application requests a book order by making a **POST** request to the `/book-order` resource of the **Order Service**. The Order microservice handles this request by sending a GET operation to fetch information about the requested book with its ISBN number from the **Book Service**. If the requested book is available in the warehouse, the Order microservice creates an order for the customer and returns a 201 response to the **ShopFrontUI** or the mobile application.

Let's now move on and have a look at the benefits of REST.

## Benefits of REST

The REST architectural style for inter-service communication has the following benefits:

- HTTP is supported by every platform and language
- Many different clients such as scripts, browsers, and applications are supported
- Scalable
- Support is provided for redirecting, caching, using different representations, and identifying resources
- Support is provided for XML, but also other formats such as JSON and Atom

Let's now have a look at another RPC system provided by Google.

# Google Remote Procedure Calls

**Google Remote Procedure Calls (gRPC)** is an open source **Remote Procedure Call (RPC)** system used to provide communication between microservices. gRPC is based on the HTTP/2 protocol. It also provides various features such as authentication, blocking or non-blocking bindings, bidirectional streaming and flow control, and cancellation and timeouts. gRPC supports various programming languages such as C++, C#, Dart, Go, Java, Node.js, Objective-C, PHP, Python, and Ruby. It provides cross-platform clients and server bindings for any language.

Google started the gRPC protocol to communicate between modules of a distributed microservice-based application within the same intranet or on the same server, thereby reducing HTTP REST calls. In gRPC-based communication, the service client directly calls the methods of the server application on a different machine. This is similar to local method calls for the same application on the same server.

We have to define the methods in a service. These methods can be called remotely using their parameters and return types, as in any RPC system. Similarly, on the server side, we have to implement the same methods. We also have to run a gRPC server to handle all the requests coming from clients. The client has a stub implementation, just as the server has all the methods and their implementations.

The following diagram illustrates the gRPC system:

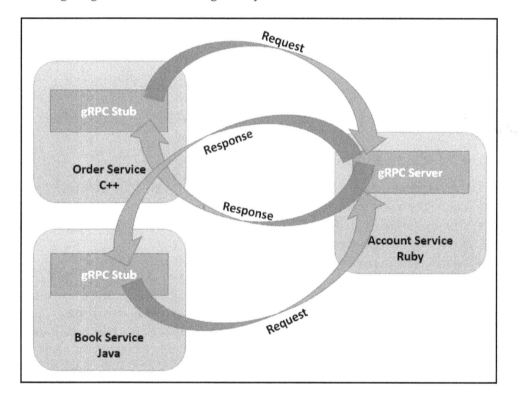

As you can see in the preceding diagram, the gRPC client and server are talking to each other. The client gRPC and the server gRPC have different languages. Therefore, a gRPC-based protocol supports various environments and languages. You can learn more about the gRPC system at https://grpc.io/.

In the following section, we'll have a look at another system used to provide inter-service communication between microservices.

# Apache Thrift

When designing a server, there are a lot of repetitive and tedious tasks that you usually have to do all by yourself. These include the following processes:

- Designing a protocol
- Serializing and deserializing messages on the protocol with code
- Dealing with sockets
- Managing concurrency
- Dealing with clients in different languages

Apache Thrift gets rid of all these excessive tasks. It can carry out all of these automatically after you provide a description of the functions you want to deliver from your server to the client and their parameters. This allows Apache Thrift to generate code in accordance with any choice of language.

The Apache Thrift framework works as follows:

- First, it provides an interface definition language that is free from any specific language and its restrictions.
- With this interface definition language, a compiler is also required to produce server and client codes.
- Apache Thrift provides compiler-generated client code and compiler-generated server code. In the compiler-generated client code, the parameters passed over the functions are converted to a binary format so that they can be transported over the network. This process is commonly known as **marshalling**.
- In the compiler-generated server code, the functions of the client code are implemented. The parameters that were converted to binary in the client-side code are received by the server-side code, which converts them back to their original language objects and passes them through the function. This process is commonly known as **unmarshalling**.
- The result of the compiler-generated server code is then converted to binary and sent through the wire over the network to the compiler-generated client code where it is converted back to the original language objects and shown over the user interface.

Most synchronous communications are one-to-one. In synchronous one-to-one communication, you can also use multiple instances of a service to scale the service. However, if you do, you have to use a load-balancing mechanism at the client side. Each service contains meta-information about all instances of the calling service. This information is provided by the service discovery server, an example of which is Netflix Eureka. There are several load-balancing mechanisms you can use. One of these is Netflix Ribbon, which carries out load-balancing on the client side, as illustrated in the following diagram:

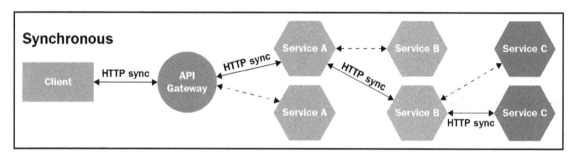

As you can see in the preceding diagram, we have multiple instances of a particular service, but the services are still communicating one-to-one. That means that each service communicates to an instance of another service. The load balancer chooses which method should be called. The following is a list of some of the most common load-balancing methods available:

- **Round-Robin**: This is the simplest method that routes requests across all the instances sequentially
- **Least Connections**: This is a method in which the request goes to the instance that has the fewest number of connections at the time
- **Weighted Round-Robin**: This is an algorithm that assigns weight to each instance and forwards the connection according to this weight
- **IP Hash**: This is a method that generates a unique hash key from the source IP address and determines which instance receives the request

Spring Cloud provides support to Netflix libraries to balance the load on the client side; you can also use Spring's RestTemplate or Feign client. Netflix Feign implements load-balancing internally.

The following code snippet performs the Feign client configuration:

```
@FeignClient(value = "ACCOUNT-SERVICE", fallback = AccountFallback.class)
public interface AccountClient {
        @GetMapping("/accounts/customer/{customerId}")
        List <Account> getAccounts(@PathVariable("customerId") Integer
customerId);
}
@Component
public class AccountFallback implements AccountClient {
        @Override
        public List <Account> getAccounts(Integer customerId) {
                List <Account> acc = new ArrayList<>();
                return acc;
        }
}
```

In the preceding code, we also configured Hystrix as a circuit breaker pattern.

In the following section, we'll discuss another approach for inter-service communication.

# Asynchronous communication

In this communication style, the client service doesn't wait for a response from another service and therefore doesn't block the thread while it is waiting. This type of communication is possible with lightweight messaging brokers. Instead of waiting for a response, the message-producer service generates a message and sends it to the broker. It only waits for an acknowledgment from the message broker about whether the message has been received or not, as shown in the following diagram:

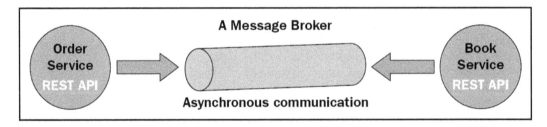

As you can see in the preceding diagram, the **Order Service** generates a message to **A Message Broker** and then forgets about it. The **Book Service** that subscribes to a topic is fed with all the messages belonging to that topic. The services don't need to know each other at all, they just need to know that messages of a certain type exist with a certain payload.

There are various tools to support lightweight messaging. All you need to do is choose one of the following message brokers to deliver your messages to consumers that run on the respective microservices:

- RabbitMQ
- Apache Kafka
- Apache ActiveMQ
- NSQ

The above tools are based on the **Advanced Message Queuing Protocol** (**AMQP**). This protocol provides messaging based on inter-service communication. The Spring Cloud Stream also provides mechanisms for building message-driven microservices using either the RabbitMQ or Apache Kafka.

Let's now turn look at messaging.

# Messaging

We can use asynchronous messaging for inter-service communication. This refers to services that communicate by exchanging messages over messaging channels. There are various messaging technologies available on the market, including message brokers such as **Apache Kafka**, **RabbitMQ**, **Apache ActiveMQ**, and **NSQ**.

# Benefits of messaging

Messaging in an asynchronous inter-service communication style has the following benefits:

- Message brokers provide an **automatic retry mechanism**. This means that if a service is not available, the message broker will send the message to that service again and retry.
- The message broker also removes the coupling between services in inter-service communication. In our example, this means that the Book Service doesn't need to be available at the time the Order Service sends the message.
- Messaging also provides flexible client-service interactions.

# Drawbacks of messaging

Messaging in an asynchronous inter-service communication style has the following drawbacks:

- The **Message Broker must not fail**. If it fails, the whole application will not function.
- The **message schema must be defined** within the message broker for all services. If there are any changes in the format of the message, this can affect the functioning of the application.
- **Transaction management** is another caveat of the messaging approach for inter-service communication. We can use **Two-Phase Commit** to manage the transactions for a distributed application, but this is not always supported.

Transactional messaging can be used to overcome these issues. We'll look at this more closely in the following section.

# Transactional messaging

Let's modify a simple messaging communication process to overcome some of its weaknesses, as discussed in the preceding section. This modified process is illustrated in the following diagram:

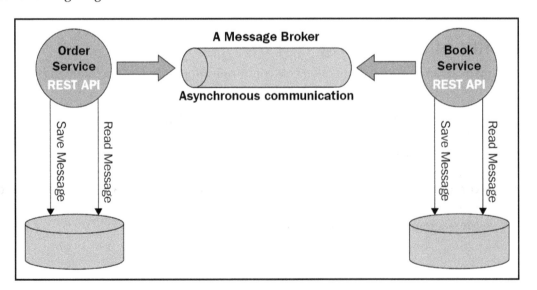

As you can see, the service doesn't send a message directly to the message broker; it first stores it in a service's local database. Similarly, on the receiving service side, the message also gets stored in the receiver's local database before being processed by the message broker.

Transactional messaging provides the following benefits:

- **Two-Phase Commit** isn't required because we are writing messages in the local database, rather than sending them directly to the **Message Broker**. We can use the same transaction as used by the service layer. If the service layer fails, the transaction is rolled back with the message as well. This approach removes the need to send a message to the message broker.
- If the **Message Broker** fails for any reason, no messages are lost, because we are writing in the database on both the sending and receiving side. While the message broker is repaired, we can send messages from the message database.

The one **drawback** of transactional messaging is that it **is quite complex to set up** for a distributed application because it means there are extra jobs for writing messages in sending and receiving databases. Jobs should also be written to read unprocessed messages.

We have now seen both simple messaging and transactional messaging used in an asynchronous inter-service communication context. So, let's now look at two further properties of the asynchronous communication style; they are as follows:

- One-to-one service communication
- One-to-many service communication

Let's take a closer look at these properties.

# One-to-one service communication

In this communication approach, each service client request is processed by one instance of a service. There are the following kinds of one-to-one interaction:

- **Notification**: In this case, a **Client** sends a request to the **Service**; the **Client** does not wait for a reply from that **Service**
- **Request/async response**: Here, a **Client** sends a request to a **Service**, which replies asynchronously; the client does not block the thread while waiting and it is designed with the assumption that the response may not immediately arrive

The following diagram demonstrates one-to-one asynchronous service communication:

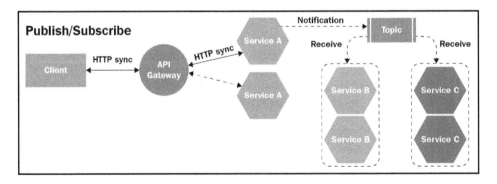

As you can see in the preceding diagram, each service has only one instance and the services are communicating through the message broker queue.

# One-to-many service communication

In this communication approach, each request from a service client is processed by multiple service instances. There are the following kinds of one-to-many interaction available:

- **Publish/subscribe**: In this approach, a **Client** publishes a notification message to the message broker and this notification message is consumed by zero or more interested services

- **Publish/async responses**: In this approach, a **Client** publishes a request message and then waits for a certain amount of time for responses from interested services

Take a look at the following diagram, which demonstrates one-to-many asynchronous service communication:

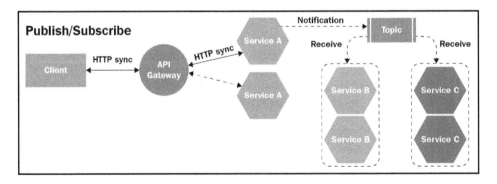

In the preceding diagram, you can see that there are multiple instances of each service. Here, a client service publishes a notification message as a topic and this topic is consumed by one or more instances of the interested services.

We can also use events instead of messages for asynchronous inter-service communication. We'll look closer at event-based communication in the following section.

# Event-based communication

Event-based communication is very similar to messaging. Instead of sending messages, the service instead generates events. Take a look at the following diagram:

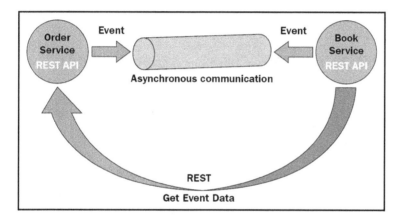

As you can see, the Order Service generates an event. This is a signal that something has happened, such as an order for a book being generated. The services that are interested in this type of event, *order generated*, send a call to the **Order Service**.

In event-based communication, there is no need for a particular message structure from the message broker. We can also use this approach with transactional messaging to avoid Two-Phase Commit.

We have now looked at multiple approaches for inter-service communication. Deciding which one to use can be difficult because there are no hard and fast rules as to which ones are better. However, it can be useful to look at the individual situation and consider which is most suitable.

With that in mind, let's now have a look at the following patterns, which can be used to design an event-driven architecture for a distributed application:

- The **Command Query Responsibility Segregation (CQRS)** pattern
- The Event Sourcing Modeling pattern
- The Eventual Consistency pattern

# The Command Query Responsibility Segregation pattern

CQRS is an architecture design in which reading and writing are divided into different sections. This means that any given method will either be performing an action via a command or reading and processing data via a query.

In a **Domain-Driven Design (DDD)** application, it is recommended that you divide the application into two layers: the command side and the query side. The command side includes the write method and contains an Order Aggregate. The Order Aggregate only contains the command methods and an Order Repository, which edits the Order Aggregate. Another repository is formed for the read method and its sole task is to read and return the correct data as specified by the query entered.

CQRS can be implemented in a number of ways. One common method is to use the same database for both the read and write models. The write model edits and updates the database, whereas the read model runs the user's query through the database, retracts the correct information or data from the database, and presents it over the user interface for the user. However, some applications can run more efficiently if two separate storage spaces are used for the different methods. In this approach, the write method updates one database, which then updates the read database. The read method runs queries and retracts data from the read database.

CQRS designs usually have the following features in common:

- Task-based UI
- Command processing
- Synchronous or asynchronous
- Domain events

The following diagram illustrates the CQRS pattern:

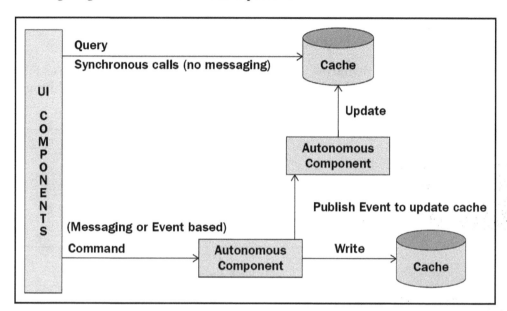

As you can see in the preceding diagram, in the CQRS pattern we split the application into two parts: the command side and the query side. On the command side, the application handles requests such as create, update, and delete, which are responsible for changing the application's object states. On the query side, the application handles queries to fetch business data to be viewed at the frontend of the application.

The CQRS pattern improves the separation of concerns by dividing the application into two separate parts. Let's now take a look at another event-based model pattern.

# The Event Sourcing Model pattern

Event sourcing is the process of modeling your system around events. By events, we mean the current state and the changes that have occurred to that state at different stages. An object is maintained by storing a sequence of events showing the changes that have been made to the state. Every new change is appended to that sequence. Almost every application can be modeled in the event-sourcing style. A process is explained not with database tables, but as a series of events, like a story.

All events are maintained in an event store, which acts as a database. However, any user can subscribe to an event with the help of an API. When they are subscribed, the event can then be provided to the subscriber through an event store. The event store is what keeps the whole event-driven microservice architecture up and running.

In this pattern, we have to define event classes. In our example, these might be as follows: **OrderCreated**, **OrderCanceled**, **OrderApproved**, **OrderRejected**, and **OrderShipped**. The following diagram shows how to create an order for a book:

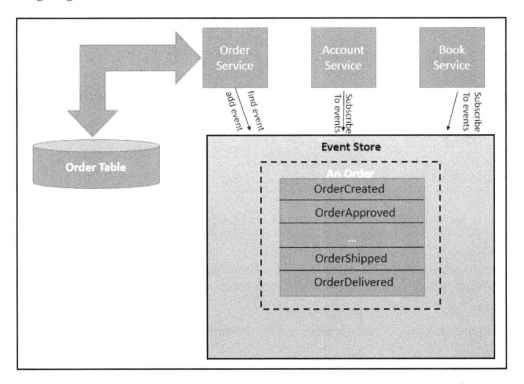

As you can see in the preceding diagram, the **Order Service** creates an order for a book and inserts a row into the **Order Table**. It also publishes the event to the event store, where other services subscribe to events. For example, the **Account Service** subscribes to events regarding customer management and the **Book Service** subscribes to events regarding inventory management

In an event-based architecture, you can update an order as follows:

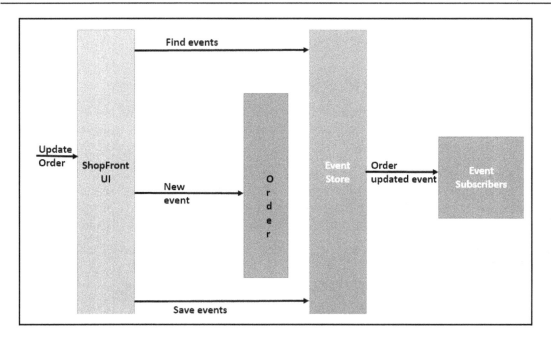

As you can see in the preceding diagram, a customer generates an **update order** request. The event source receives this order and the application finds the order using *find the event by order ID*. It then updates the order and saves it to the event source. All subscribers are notified when the order is updated to the event source.

# Benefits

The benefits of event sourcing are as follows:

- **Auditing accuracy:** Auditing is a tiring and tedious task and there is often a risk of it being incomplete or incorrect. However, with the event-driven microservice architecture in place, audit logging becomes automatic as it is carried out with every event change in the model. This makes auditing 100% accurate.

- **Easy temporal queries:** With the event-driven microservice architecture, the history of all the event changes is maintained by the application itself. This makes implementing temporal queries simple.

- **Simple reports:** Generating a complex business report takes up a lot of time and energy. An event-driven microservices architecture makes the task of generating reports simple by providing all the historical data required.

Let's now move on and take a look at an alternative pattern.

## The Eventual Consistency pattern

We have already looked at an event-sourcing-based system using CQRS that has two parts: one for commands and one for queries. Having separate models raises questions about data consistency for models used at the frontend.

Eventual Consistency is a consistency model that can be applied to an event-based distributed application to achieve high availability. If no update is made to the system's domain, it will return the last updated value for that domain. Eventual Consistency is also known as Optimistic Replication, and it is commonly used in distributed systems.

## Domain-specific protocol

In a microservice architecture, we can use a domain-specific protocol for inter-service communication. There are various domain-specific protocols available, which include the following:

- Email protocols, such as **SMTP** and **IMAP**
- Media streaming protocols, such as **RTMP**, **HLS**, and **HDS**

You can choose which protocol is most appropriate for you depending on your application. For example, REST communication uses the HTTP/HTTPS protocol.

## Summary

Microservices must communicate using an inter-process communication mechanism. In this chapter, we have learned about the multiple approaches for inter-service communication. We have discussed two approaches: the synchronous communication style and the asynchronous communication style. We then discussed one-to-one inter-service communication, which uses a single receiver, and one-to-many inter-service communication, which uses multiple receivers. After that, we looked at various technologies that provide inter-service communication mechanisms.

In the next chapter, *Service Registry and Discovery*, we'll discuss how to use the External API Gateway to provide extended flexibility, an approach that calls services and variations, patterns, and use cases.

# Service Registry and Discovery

**5**

In previous chapters, we discussed a variety of points about the microservice architecture, but this chapter is all about how to discover a service. In `Chapter 4`, *Inter-Service Communication*, we discussed how services communicate with each other and looked at different aspects of communication within a microservice architecture.

As you know, we require both the IP address and the port for any communication between services when using either the REST API or the Apache Thrift API. However, it is possible to change the IP address, so how can we ensure that service communication remains stable? In this chapter, we will explore the solution to this problem and discuss other issues related to service discovery.

After reading this chapter, you will be able to diagnose service discovery issues related to microservice REST APIs and the service client.

This chapter will cover the following topics:

- The need for service discovery in microservice architecture
- Service discovery patterns:
    - The client-side discovery pattern
    - The server-side discovery pattern
- Microservice registry and discovery with Eureka:
    - Implementing the Service Registry with Eureka
    - Implementing the Eureka Discovery server

Let's get started!

# Technical Requirements

You will be required to have Spring Boot 2.0, Java 8, Spring Tool Suite Version 3.9.5 release, Maven, and JMeter installed to follow the procedure.

The code files of this chapter can be found on GitHub:
`https://github.com/PacktPublishing/Hands-On-Microservices-Monitoring-and-Testin g/tree/master/Chapter05`

Check out the following video to see the code in action:
`http://bit.ly/2ELYD5O`

# The need for service discovery in microservice architecture

In traditional or old-fashioned application architecture, IP addresses and ports are mainly static and fixed so that they can be easily managed for client applications. In a static, configuration-based application, each service is deployed at the same location and only rarely do we need to change the location of the services. However, in the case of cloud-based microservices applications, IP addresses and ports are very difficult, and sometimes even impossible, to manage.

In the microservice architecture, we cannot guarantee that there will be static configuration because microservices are independently deployable and individual teams work on individual microservices; each team can deploy and scale their microservices independently. More services and instances may also be added to the system to provide scalability to the distributed application. Because of this scaling, service locations can change frequently, so locations cannot be thought of as static. This means that a more dynamic configuration is needed for the microservice architecture.

Let's assume that we have many instances of several services on a different server. Due to the dynamic location of these services, it is much more difficult to manage service discovery in the client application. This problem is illustrated in the following diagram:

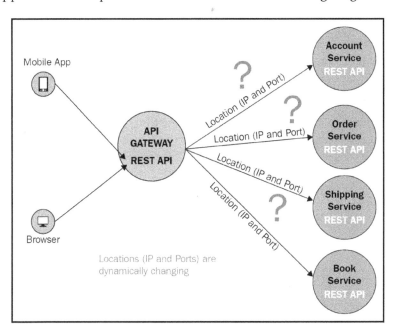

In the preceding diagram, you can see that all service instances have dynamic IP addresses and ports. However, the service clients and the API Gateway, which we will discuss in the next chapter, need to be able to communicate with the services. The client code, or the API Gateway, therefore need a better mechanism to find services—one which doesn't require the hardcoded location of a service. In the following section, we'll take a look at the service discovery patterns.

# Service discovery patterns

In a microservice architecture, it is very important to implement service discovery. This enables client applications to search for services without a hardcoded network location. We can implement a service discovery pattern in two ways: through client-side discovery and server-side discovery. We'll go through these two service discovery patterns in detail in the following sections.

# The client-side discovery pattern

In a microservice-based application, services need to communicate with one another to carry out a business task. In a monolithic application, communication between services is very easy, because all services are typically part of the same application. However, in a distributed system, the services are *not* part of the same application. Instead, services run on separate, independent virtual machines or containers. These have well-known locations (hosts and ports), that change if the application is scaled up or down. This is where service discovery comes in.

In client-side discovery, a client service finds the location of other service instances by querying a Service Registry. The client is also responsible for managing load balancing requests across services. The Service Registry is a database for microservice instances. On the client side, we have to use an algorithm to select one of the available instances using a few parameters.

The following diagram illustrates the client-side service discovery pattern:

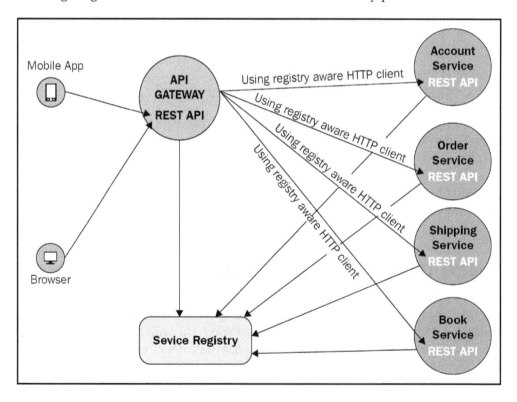

As you can see, the client service itself registers with the registry server. Other microservices also register with the same registry server. All instances of services are registered with the specific location on the registry server. The client service uses the service name with which it is registered, and is removed from the **Service Registry** when the instance terminates. The service instance's registration is typically refreshed periodically using a heartbeat mechanism.

This service discovery pattern has various advantages and disadvantages. The advantages are as follows:

- This pattern is very simple and straightforward because there are no moving parts related to the distributed application, except the registry server
- You can apply more intelligence on the client side to make load balancing decisions

The client-side discovery pattern also has the following disadvantages:

- This approach couples the client code with the registry server code
- You have to implement discovery logic for each service because the services may use different programming languages

Netflix OSS provides a client-side discovery pattern called Netflix Eureka. Netflix Eureka is a Service Registry that provides a REST API to manage service-instance registration and send queries to available instances. Netflix also provides another component called Netflix Ribbon, which is an IPC client that works with Eureka to load balance requests across available service instances. We will discuss Eureka in more depth later.

First, let's have a look at another approach: the server-side service discovery pattern.

# The server-side discovery pattern

In the server-side discovery pattern, the client isn't aware of the Service Registry. The client service requests a service using a load balancer, which then queries the Service Registry.

The AWS **Elastic Load Balancer** (**ELB**) is one example of server-side discovery. It is commonly used as a load balancer for external traffic from the internet. It manages the load between a set of registered Amazon **Elastic Compute Cloud** (**EC2**) instances or Amazon **EC2 Container Service** (**ECS**) containers. Other examples include HTTP servers and load balancers such as NGINX Plus.

In the server-side service discovery pattern, the client doesn't need to worry about managing the code or algorithm for load balancing and discovering services. Instead, we can use a separate load balancer server.

The following diagram illustrates server-side service discovery:

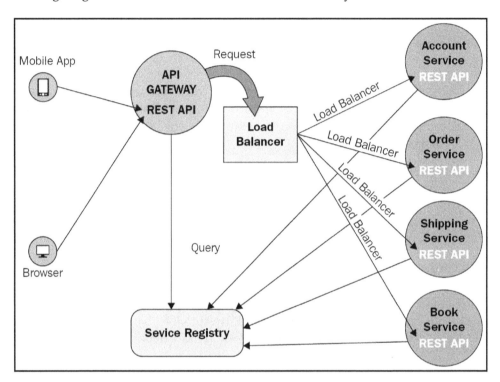

As you can see in the preceding diagram, this approach uses a **Load Balancer** server that is separate from the client service. The client service makes a request directly to the load balancer, which queries the **Service Registry** and then finds a service.

The server-side service discovery pattern has various advantages and disadvantages. Some of the advantages include the following:

- In this approach, the client service doesn't require the complex logic of searching for services or load balancing traffic
- There is no need to implement discovery logic for each programming language and framework used by a service client
- Some cloud environments, such as AWS Elastic load balancer, provide this functionality for free

This approach also has the following disadvantages:

- The load balancer needs to be a highly available system, so you have to set it up and manage it carefully
- The load balancer could be a single point of failure, so it needs to be replicated for availability and capacity
- The load balancer server must support important protocols such as HTTP, gRPC, and Thrift
- It has more network rounds than the client-side service discovery pattern

In the following section, we'll look at how to implement a microservice registry using Netflix's Eureka.

# Microservice registry and discovery with Eureka

A Service Registry is a database of the locations of service instances. The service instances are registered with the registry service upon startup and are de-registered automatically upon shutdown. Netflix provides a registry service server, which is Eureka. Spring Boot provides integration with the Netflix API, so we can easily implement a microservice registry using Netflix's Eureka server.

The client service, or external routers, makes a query to find the available instances of a service. The registry server provides all of the available instances of the requested service. Take a look at the following diagram, which shows Service Registry and discovery with Eureka:

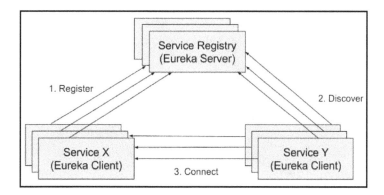

As you can see, all services register with the Eureka server to make themselves available. In the following section, we'll look at how to register services with Eureka.

# Implementing Service Registry with Eureka

We can use the Eureka registry server with Spring Cloud because it integrates with Netflix. First, add the following Maven dependency into your application's pom.xml file:

```
<dependency>
        <groupId>org.springframework.cloud</groupId>
        <artifactId>spring-cloud-starter-eureka-server</artifactId>
</dependency>
```

Let's create a service, the Account Service, and register it with the Eureka server. The application class of the Account Service in Spring Boot will look as follows:

```
package com.dineshonjava.bookshop.accountservice;

import org.springframework.boot.SpringApplication;
import org.springframework.boot.autoconfigure.SpringBootApplication;
import org.springframework.cloud.netflix.eureka.EnableEurekaClient;

@EnableEurekaClient
@SpringBootApplication
public class AccountServiceApplication {
  public static void main(String[] args) {
    SpringApplication.run(AccountServiceApplication.class, args);
  }
}
```

As you can see in the preceding code, the @EnableEurekaClient annotation activates the Netflix EurekaClient implementation. This Account Service registers itself with the Eureka server, which makes it available. Take a look at the following YML configuration file for this Account Service application:

```
spring:
 application:
 name: account-service


server:
 port: 1111


eureka:
```

```
client:
service-url:
default-zone: ${EUREKA_URI:http://localhost:8761/eureka}
instance:
prefer-ip-address: true
```

As you can see, the service name is `account-service`, and it will run on port `1111`. This service registers itself with the Eureka server running on `http://localhost:8761/eureka`.

In the following section, we will implement the Eureka server with Spring Boot.

# Implementing the Eureka Discovery server

It is very simple to implement the Eureka server application using Spring Boot; just use the following code:

```
package com.dineshonjava.bookshop.eurekaserver;

import org.springframework.boot.SpringApplication;
import org.springframework.boot.autoconfigure.SpringBootApplication;
importorg.springframework.cloud.netflix.eureka.server.EnableEurekaServer;


@EnableEurekaServer
@SpringBootApplication
public class EurekaServerApplication {


        public static void main(String[] args) {
SpringApplication.run(EurekaServerApplication.class, args);
        }
}
```

As you can see in the preceding code, the Eureka server is a small Spring Boot application. The `@EnableEurekaServer` annotation provides Netflix's Eureka registry server. Take a look at the following Eureka server application configuration file for more information:

```
server:
  port: 8761


eureka:
  instance:
    hostname: localhost
  client:
```

```
    registerWithEureka: false
    fetchRegistry: false
    serviceUrl:
      defaultZone:
  http://${eureka.instance.hostname}:${server.port}/eureka/
```

This server application uses port 8761.

Now, let's take a look at the following screenshot:

| Instances currently registered with Eureka | | | |
|---|---|---|---|
| **Application** | **AMIs** | **Availability Zones** | **Status** |
| ACCOUNT-SERVICE | n/a (1) | (1) | UP (1) - MRNDTHTMOBL0002.timesgroup.com:account-service:6060 |

As you can see, the **ACCOUNT-SERVICE** has now been successfully registered with the Eureka server. You can find the complete code for this process using the GitHub URL for this book (https://github.com/PacktPublishing/Hands-On-Microservices-Monitoring-and-Testing).

# Summary

Service discovery and registry are key parts of a microservice-based application, because locations of service instances are always changing. We can implement service discovery using two approaches: client-side service discovery and server-side service discovery. In this chapter, we used the Eureka Discovery server and registered a client application using Spring Boot, Spring Cloud, and Netflix Eureka.

In Chapter 6, *External API Gateway*, we'll discuss how to use an API gateway to provide the common interface of communication. We'll also take a look at an approach for implementing API gateway patterns and their use cases.

# External API Gateway

# 6

In previous chapters, we learned a lot about microservices, such as how to design, build, and deploy them; we also looked at how multiple microservices communicate with each other in a distributed system. In addition to this, we have discussed the benefits and drawbacks of using microservices. Regardless of the associated challenges, utilizing microservice-based architecture is the ideal choice when working with a complex and cloud-native application.

Using an external API gateway to provide extended flexibility, we will now discuss an approach to calling services and their various techniques, patterns, and use cases. In this chapter, we will explore the topic of building microservices using an API gateway. The reader will become familiar with how an API gateway helps us manage APIs, and also provides a way for an application's clients to interact with microservices.

In a microservice architecture, an application is built with many microservices that are each exposed to a set of typically fine-grained endpoints. However, in a monolithic application, there is only one set of endpoints, with the load balancer distributing the traffic among them. In the case of microservices, we have several sets of endpoints, so we can use an API gateway for client-to-application communication. This chapter will therefore cover the following points:

- Introducing an API gateway
- The benefits and drawbacks of an API gateway
- Building an API gateway
- Performance and scalability

- Service invocations
- Service discovery
- Handling partial failures
- Using the Spring Cloud Netflix Zuul proxy
- MuleSoft

Let's move on and explore these topics in detail.

# Technical Requirements

You will be required to have Spring Boot 2.0, Java 8, Spring Tool Suite Version 3.9.5 release, Maven, and JMeter installed to follow the procedure.

The code files of this chapter can be found on GitHub:
`https://github.com/PacktPublishing/Hands-On-Microservices-Monitoring-and-Testing/tree/master/Chapter06`

Check out the following video to see the code in action:
`http://bit.ly/2CEhHA2`

# Introducing an API gateway

In our online bookshop application, we have several diverse clients such as mobile, desktop, and laptop. Consequently, we have to develop the native client for this application. Let's imagine there is an order details page that displays order information about a book, as well as the details of the customer who purchased it.

The following services are required in order to obtain such order details:

- **Order Service**: This provides information about order details and order history
- **Account Service**: This provides information about the customer
- **Book Service**: This provides information about books and their availability in the product catalog
- **Shipping Service**: This provides details about shipping ordered books
- Note that the application may have many more services available

Suppose you choose to build an application with a monolithic software architecture. In this case, all the previously mentioned modules will be a part of your application, meaning the application's client fetches order details by making a single REST call (for example, `GET api.dineshonjava.com/bookshop/order/{orderId}`) to that monolithic application. In the case of a clustered application, a load balancer routes all requests to the N number of identical instances of that monolithic application. The application would fetch order details for all data - such as book information, customer information, shipping information, and so on - from various tables and then return the findings as a response to the application's client.

However, if you choose to build an application with a microservice software architecture, you need to build your application as a set of microservices. In microservice-based architecture, all modules such as Order Service, Account Service, Book Service, and Shipping Service are built as separate and independent deployable artifacts. In this case, the multiple microservices each have an order details page. Here, an application's client interacts with the microservices to fetch order details as usual; however, each independent service will expose a set of endpoints for separate VMs or containers.

You will also need to decide on a method of client-to-application communication. This is necessary because the application is not a single artifact that has all of the modules already included. In this chapter, we will discuss the following two approaches to client-to-application communication:

- Client-to-microservice communication
- API gateways

Let's start with client-to-microservice communication and see how to interact with a set of microservices in order to fetch order details.

# Client-to-microservice communication

When it comes to client-to-microservice communication, an application's client calls each of the microservices directly using the public endpoint (`https://serviceName.api.dineshonjava.name`) of that microservice. In the case of a clustered microservice, a URL would map to the load balance of a microservice.

The following diagram illustrates client-to-microservice communication:

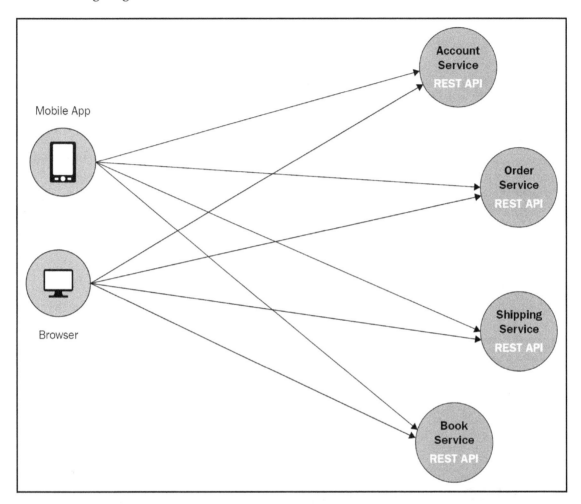

As you can see in the preceding diagram, the mobile and browser clients make requests to each of the services in order to retrieve order details. This approach has many challenges and limitations.

# Drawbacks

Let's first take a look at the limitations of the client-to-microservice approach:

- **Network discrimination**: The client has to call several (sometimes hundreds) of microservices in order to render a page. This is possible with a LAN, but in the case of a public network, it could become inefficient. It would also be very difficult when using a mobile network.
- **Complex client code**: For this approach, we have to write code for numerous REST calls for many microservices, making the client code much more complex.
- **Protocol diversity**: Some clients might use protocols that are not web-friendly. Suppose one microservice is using Apache Thrift's binary RPC and another is using gRPC or the AMQP messaging protocol. None of these protocols are web-friendly, so a browser cannot use them properly. An application should use protocols such as HTTP and WebSocket outside a firewall.
- **Refactoring microservices**: Further enhancement of services (such as merging two services or splitting a service into two or more) is extremely difficult because an application's client interacts directly with the services.

Due to these limitations, we never recommend that a client application takes a direct approach when using microservices. This is especially the case when serving an external client application; in such a case, we have to provide a common interface service to the client, such as Facade design, to interact with all microservices. In the next section, we will discuss how to use an API gateway as an alternative.

# Using an API gateway

As a best practice, a client must not have information about your microservice hosts and ports. All clients must be aware of the single entry point to all microservices. In this case, we have to implement an API gateway that provides a single entry point for clients. This is a much better approach than direct client-to-service communication.

An API gateway is an edge server that provides services to a client that is similar to the Facade pattern from object-oriented design. The API gateway hides the diversity of protocols from multiple background microservices and instead provides a common API for each client and microservice. An API gateway is responsible for request routing, composition, and protocol translation. They may also have other functionalities, such as authentication, monitoring, load balancing, caching, request shaping and management, and static response handling.

The following diagram shows how an API gateway typically fits into an example architecture:

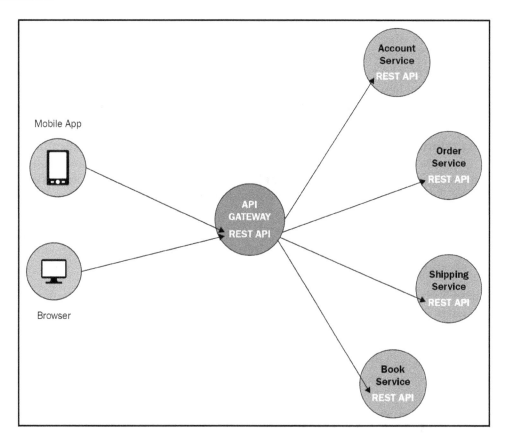

In the preceding diagram, we can see that all clients (such as mobiles and browsers) don't call a microservice directly. Instead, all requests from clients must first go through the API gateway. After this, the API gateway then routes the client's requests to the appropriate microservice. An API gateway handles the requests in the following two ways:

- By proxying or routing requests to the appropriate microservice
- By scattering them to multiple microservices; here, the gateway aggregates the results from multiple microservices and sends them to the client—for example, the API gateway provides a custom endpoint for the book details (/orderDetails?orderId=1212XX212), and then fetches them from multiple microservices such as the Account Service, Book Service, Shipping Service, and Order Service, before forwarding the aggregated results to the client

The API gateway can translate between protocols such as HTTP and WebSocket, as well as web-unfriendly protocols that are used internally. You can also design an API gateway per client type. For example, a browser can use an API gateway and a mobile client uses an API gateway exclusively for mobile. Similarly, Netflix uses various API gateways due to its vast variety of clients, including televisions, set-top boxes, smartphones, gaming systems, tablets, and so on. Due to the availability of a diverse range of devices, a one-size-fit-all API does not always work well.

The following diagram illustrates using multiple API gateways across a diverse range of devices:

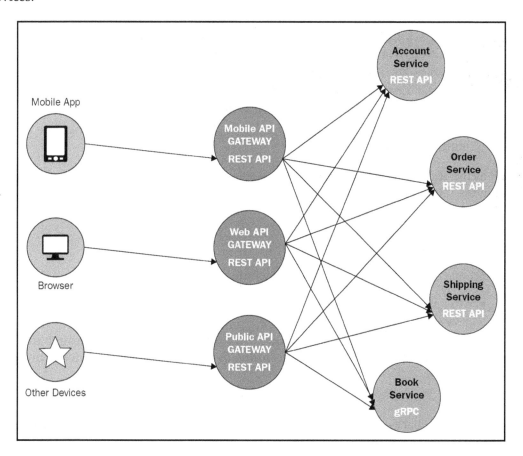

In the preceding diagram, **Mobile App** clients use a **Mobile API Gateway,** while **Browser** clients use a **Web API Gateway**. Other devices such as set-top boxes and gaming systems use another **Public API Gateway.**

Let's now look at the benefits and drawbacks of using an API gateway.

# Benefits

Using an API gateway has the following benefits:

- It hides the complexity of background microservices from clients
- Clients don't need to worry about resolving the location of each microservice instance
- It provides a custom API for each client
- It reduces unnecessary network round-trips, in other words, when a client makes a single request for specific data from multiple microservices
- It provides the flexibility to merge two or more services as a single service, or even split a single service into two or more services
- It supports protocol diversity as well as client device diversity
- It can centralize cross-cutting concerns, such as security, monitoring, rate limiting, and so on

As well as the above benefits, using an API gateway also has some drawbacks, which we'll look at in the following section.

# Drawbacks

The limitations of the API gateway pattern include the following:

- API gateways must be created as Edge applications, which in turn must be developed, deployed, and managed
- It might increase response time due to additional network calls through the API gateway—this is not as time-consuming as the client-to-microservice approach, however
- It could become a single point of failure if the proper measures are not taken

Despite these drawbacks, the API gateway approach is widely used by most real-world applications.

# Building an API gateway

In this section, we will look at how to build an API Gateway. In the microservice-based architecture, the API gateway is just like a router that routes client requests to the appropriate microservice. So, while we build an API gateway application, we need to consider the various best practices in order to avoid any design issues. We will discuss potential design issues for the API gateway in this section.

## API gateway performance and scalability

The performance and scalability of an API gateway application are very important because they are both single points that all client requests pass. With that in mind, we need to consider asynchronous and non-blocking I/O platforms when building an API gateway application. There are many platforms that provide these asynchronously, including non-blocking I/O platforms such as Netty, Vertx, Spring Reactor, and JBoss Undertow.

## Building an API gateway using a reactive programming model

The reactive programming model is a much better approach than the traditional asynchronous callback approach that is often used for building an API gateway application. Here, we can use Java 8's CompletableFuture Scala's, Future, ReactiveX, Netflix's RxJava for the JVM, Spring Reactor, and many more.

## API gateway and service invocation mechanism support

In microservice-based architectures, a service can communicate to other services for a business task by using an inter-service communication mechanism, as discussed in `Chapter 4: Inter-Service Communication`. There are two approaches to inter-service communication. One approach is a synchronous mechanism, such as REST calls or Apache Thrift and gRPC. The other approach is an asynchronous mechanism, such as a message-driven or event-driven implementation, via a message broker such as JMS, AQMP, RabbitMQ, and Apache Kafka.

An API gateway will need to support a variety of communication mechanisms, but it can also translate calls between different types of protocol. Please note, however, that it must support a protocol's diversity of multiple microservice usage.

# API gateway and service discovery

In microservice-based architectures, all microservices use the IP address and port as the location of each microservice, which the API gateway needs to know in order to communicate. You could hardcoded the IP address and port of the microservice, but this is not as easy in the case of multiple instances of the same microservice. Fortunately, service discovery is a mechanism that allows you to register your microservices with a service registry server, such as Netflix's Eureka.

There are two types of discovery mechanism: **server-side discovery** and **client-side discovery**. In the client-side discovery mechanism, the API gateway must be able to query the service registry server where all microservices are registered with their locations. In the server-side discovery mechanism, the client (such as an API gateway) requests the router deployed on another server, and that router then queries the service registry server.

The client-side discovery mechanism has less overhead because it has fewer moving parts and network hops in comparison to server-side discovery, and is therefore preferable. An API gateway must be aware of the service registry mechanism being used. As the API gateway application is also registered with a registry server, such as Netflix's Eureka, let's look at the code required to register the application as follows:

```
@EnableEurekaClient
public class ApiZuulProxyApplication {
  ....
}
```

As you can see, the `@EnableEurekaClient` annotation is used to register the application to the Eureka service discovery server.

# Handling partial failures

The microservice-based application is a distributed application, but as there are many microservices that run on the cloud or different VMs, we have to design an API gateway so that it can handle the problem of partial failure. Note that, in a distributed system, one microservice calls another microservice.

It might be possible that a microservice is either responding slowly or is unavailable, but its calls are not blocked by an API gateway over its non-response. Instead, the API gateway must sometimes handle these failures.

For example, let's say an order details page also includes a shipping company's ratings generated by another rating microservice. If that rating microservice is unresponsive in the order details rendering, then the API gateway must return the rest of the order information to the client. In this case, the rating of the shipping company can either be empty or replaced by a hardcoded value. If any important microservice, such as an order service or account service, is unresponsive, the API gateway should return an error to the client.

Netflix provides a library called **Hystrix**, which is a very useful library for handling partial failure in a distributed application. Spring Cloud supports Netflix's Hystrix library, and we can easily use this with the Spring Boot-based microservice application.

In the Hystrix API, you can also set a `timeout` property that specifies the threshold for exceeding. If this timeout is reached, a circuit breaker will open and stop the client from needlessly waiting for an unresponsive service. After reaching a defined threshold for a service's error rate, Hystrix will also open the circuit breaker and all requests will fail for a specific time. You can define your logic for the Hystrix's fallback method so that the value is taken from a cache or returned from a default value.

The following code demonstrates how to use Spring Cloud with Netflix's Hystrix library to handle partial failure:

```
@Service
public class AccountServiceImpl implements AccountService {
@Autowired
          @LoadBalanced
          RestTemplate restTemplate;

          @HystrixCommand(fallbackMethod = "defaultAccount")
          public Account findAccount(Integer accountId) {
                    return
restTemplate.getForObject("http://ACCOUNT-SERVICE/account/{accountId}",
Account.class, accountId);
          }

          private Account defaultAccount(Integer accountId) {
                    return new Account(0001, "Rushika Rajput", "Noida",
"972XXX2323", "rushika.zzzz@mymail.com");
     }
}
```

In the preceding code snippet, AccountServiceImpl from our online bookshop application uses a circuit breaker to handle failures when invoking a remote service. The AccountServiceImpl class has a method, findAccount(<accountId>), that must be executed using a circuit breaker by annotating with the @HystrixCommand annotation. Another method named defaultAccount(<accountId>) is also defined as a fallback method for the circuit breaker.

The circuit breaker functionality is enabled using the @EnableCircuitBreaker annotation on the OrderServiceApplication class, as follows:

```
package com.dineshonjava.bookshop.orderservice;

    import org.springframework.boot.SpringApplication;
    import org.springframework.boot.autoconfigure.SpringBootApplication;
    import
    org.springframework.cloud.client.circuitbreaker.EnableCircuitBreaker;
    import org.springframework.cloud.netflix.eureka.EnableEurekaClient;
    import
    org.springframework.cloud.netflix.hystrix.dashboard.EnableHystrixDashboard;

    @EnableEurekaClient
    @EnableCircuitBreaker
    @EnableHystrixDashboard
    @SpringBootApplication
    public class OrderServiceApplication {

            public static void main(String[] args) {
    SpringApplication.run(OrderServiceApplication.class, args);
            }
    }
```

The preceding main class annotates using the @EnableCircuitBreaker and @EnableHystrixDashboard annotations. The @EnableCircuitBreaker annotation is used to enable a circuit breaker in the application, while the @EnableHystrixDashboard annotation provides a circuit breaker in the Hystrix dashboard.

Let's now move on to the next section and look at how to build an API gateway using Spring Cloud's Netflix Zuul proxy.

# Building an API gateway using Spring Cloud's Netflix Zuul proxy

Spring Cloud provides the Zuul proxy to build an API gateway application. The following example demonstrates how to create an API gateway application using that proxy. So, let's create a Spring Boot project with the following code:

```
<dependencies>
        <dependency>
                <groupId>org.springframework.cloud</groupId>
                <artifactId>spring-cloud-starter-netflix-
                eureka-client</artifactId>
        </dependency>
        <dependency>
                <groupId>org.springframework.cloud</groupId>
                <artifactId>spring-cloud-starter-netflix-
                zuul</artifactId>
        </dependency>

        <dependency>
                <groupId>org.springframework.boot</groupId>
                <artifactId>spring-boot-starter-
                web</artifactId>
        </dependency>
</dependencies>
```

In the preceding Maven configuration file, you can see that we have included the Web, Eureka Discovery, and Zuul starters. Let's now create the main entry-point class with @EnableZuulProxy as follows:

```
package com.dineshonjava.bookshop.apizuulproxy;
import org.springframework.boot.SpringApplication;
import org.springframework.boot.autoconfigure.SpringBootApplication;
import org.springframework.cloud.netflix.eureka.EnableEurekaClient;
import org.springframework.cloud.netflix.zuul.EnableZuulProxy;

@EnableZuulProxy
@EnableEurekaClient
@SpringBootApplication
public class ApiZuulProxyApplication {
        public static void main(String[] args) {
                SpringApplication.run(ApiZuulProxyApplication.class,
                args);
        }
}
```

As you can see in the preceding code, we have annotated this main class with three annotations: @EnableZuulProxy, @EnableEurekaClient, and @SpringBootApplication. The @SpringBootApplication annotation is responsible for auto-configuration, which enables a boot application. The @EnableEurekaClient annotation allows an API gateway to register with the service discovery, and the @EnableZuulProxy annotation enables the Zuul proxy.

The following YAML configuration file illustrates how to configure the Zuul proxy for microservices:

```
spring:
  application:
    name: API-GATEWAY

server:
  port: 8080

eureka:
  client:
    service-url:
      default-zone: ${EUREKA_URI:http://localhost:8761/eureka}
  instance:
    prefer-ip-address: true

zuul:
  ignoredServices: '*'
  prefix: /api
  routes:
    account-service:
      path: /account/**
      serviceId: ACCOUNT-SERVICE
    book-service:
      path: /book/**
      serviceId: BOOK-SERVICE
    order-service:
      path: /order/**
      serviceId: ORDER-SERVICE
    shipping-service:
      path: /shipping/**
      serviceId: SHIPPING-SERVICE
  host:
    socket-timeout-millis: 30000
```

As you can see in the preceding YAML configuration file, we have exposed services such as ACCOUNT-SERVICE, BOOK-SERVICE, ORDER-SERVICE, and SHIPPING-SERVICE through the Zuul proxy. By default, all the services registered with Eureka Server will be exposed. For this reason, we have set the `zuul.ignoredServices` property to override this default behavior and have only routed some services explicitly, as you can see with the configured services in the YAML configuration.

We have also set a common prefix for all URLs, such as /api, by setting the `zuul.prefix` property.

In the preceding configuration, we used the URL `http://localhost:8080/api/order/<orderId>`, which is forwarded to the service with the service ID, ORDER-SERVICE.

As you have seen in the preceding examples, the Zuul proxy aggregates all configured services as a single application and requests a route from the Zuul proxy to the microservices. The Zuul service can also be used to implement other functionalities for cross-cutting concerns, such as authentication and authorization, API rate limiting, and so on.

There are many external APIs available on the market that provide API management functionalities, including API rate limiting, filtering, and so on. MuleSoft is one of them.

# MuleSoft

MuleSoft is an integration platform that helps with connecting applications, data, and devices. While the company originally provided middleware and messaging services, over the years it has expanded enough to provide a fully-fledged integration platform for different companies.

MuleSoft also provides APIhub, which is like a social media platform used by developers to interact with each other, and share their ideas, updates, and information about the technology world. In this platform, developers can find all kinds of API, as it currently hosts around 13,000 of them. MuleSoft also provides a catalog of APIs and an interactive development environment where developers can run basic queries.

To those who provide the API, MuleSoft offers various tools to generate API documentation automatically, along with a publishing platform. With so many facilities available, MuleSoft is working diligently towards the betterment of technological society, as well as providing a platform for developers everywhere to come together.

MuleSoft saves you from the tedious and sometimes hectic task of data integration and does this work for you diligently and efficiently. Tools and services offered by MuleSoft include:

- **API Designer**: This is a web-based tool which contains a console and a scripting notebook for JavaScript.
- **API Manager**: This is a management tool which allows organizations to manage users, traffics, and service level agreements.
- **Anypoint Studio**: This is a graphical design environment for building and editing integrations.
- **API Portal**: This is a portal which offers developers different kinds of documents, tutorials, and code snippets.
- **API Analytics**: This is an analytics tool which allows the user to track the specifications of an API, including its performance, usage, and reliability. It also offers a dashboard and charts.

# Summary

In microservice-based architectures, many microservices run with their own IP addresses and ports; consequently, it is very difficult to manage the location of each instance for clients. The diversity of protocols is another concern for clients. As a result, it makes sense to implement an API gateway service that provides a single entry point to all microservices without the need to remember the location of each microservice. An API gateway is responsible for request routing, composition, and protocol translation.

In *Chapter 6: Testing of Microservices*, we'll explore various approaches and strategies for testing microservices.

# 7
# Testing of Microservices

In this chapter, the user will explore various strategies for testing microservices, microservice input headers, and payload details. We will discuss different testing approaches for microservice applications within this chapter.

A microservice architecture consists of small, independently deployable, and single responsibility-focused services. These services can be aggregated together to make a complete business application. A single instance of a microservice must serve a single business responsibility in your business application. These services are independent of each other, and you can easily test and deploy each one individually.

This chapter will cover the following topics:

- Testing strategies for microservices
- Unit testing
- Integration testing
- Component testing
- Contract testing
- End-to-end testing
- UI/functional testing

Let's take a look at these topics in detail in the upcoming sections.

# Technical Requirements

You will be required to have Spring Boot 2.0, Java 8, Spring Tool Suite Version 3.9.5 release, Maven, and JMeter installed to follow the procedure.

The code files of this chapter can be found on GitHub:
```
https://github.com/PacktPublishing/Hands-On-Microservices-Monitoring-and-
Testing/tree/master/Chapter07
```

Check out the following video to see the code in action:
`http://bit.ly/2S14cuv`

# Testing strategies for microservices

Software industries are now using the microservice-based architecture for every new development. In addition, most companies are moving from monolithic to microservice-based architectures. Consequently, each microservice must be tested before it communicates with other microservices.

As we know, a microservice is an architectural style that develops a single application with a suite of services. These services are independent deployable, have different data storage methods, and can also be used in different languages. They either have a bare minimum of dependencies or zero dependencies with centralized management. These services are built around business capability and can also be deployed by containers. Sometimes, this characteristic of the microservice style creates complexity for testers trying to test a microservice end-to-end.

# The testing pyramid strategy

The traditional approach to the testing pyramid is shown in the following diagram:

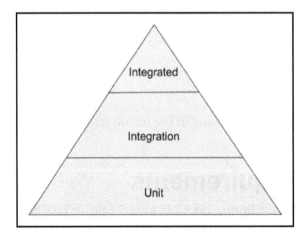

As you can see in the diagram, the testing pyramid approach is extremely efficient for a monolithic application. For a long time, this strategy was used by most enterprises in the software world. However, in a microservice world, this approach is not much suitable for the best way of testing a microservice-based application. Because the biggest complexity is not within the microservice itself, but in how microservices interacts with other microservices. But the above approach much focuses on the unit testing rather than integration testing. That is why such an approach can be harmful to the microservice application.

# The testing honeycomb strategy

In the microservice architecture, having too many unit tests with a small definition for each microservice is not the best choice. Each microservice is bound with a single business capability, not a whole business. This might simply be a small part of the business scope, so it is not worth writing too many unit test cases for a microservice. A better way of structuring our tests for microservices would be through the testing honeycomb, as seen in the following diagram:

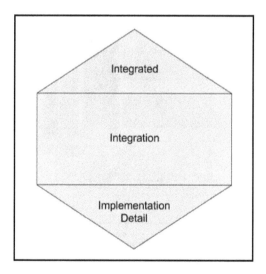

As you can see in the preceding diagram, the integration part is greater than other parts that means our main focus will be on integration testing, rather than unit and integrated testing. It is worth noting that there are very few implementation detail tests and integrated tests.

Let's discuss unit testing in the next section.

# Unit testing

When it comes to testing units for microservices, unit test cases only cover a single microservice. We could have a number of unit test cases for a microservice, where the unit test depends on what language we are using in the development of that microservice. It also depends on the framework being used in development.

A unit can consist of a line of code, a method, or a class. Unit testing refers to testing a particular unit for any bugs or issues. Optimally, the smaller the unit is, the better it is, because this allows testing on a more granular level, and gives a more accurate view of how well the overall code is performing. The most important factor of unit testing is that, by running many small tests, instead of one big test, you can complete the testing process in a matter of seconds or minutes, instead of hours, depending on the size of the code. See the following diagram showing a microservice that has unit tests in accordance with the number of units:

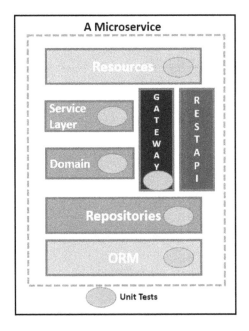

The preceding diagram is concerned with unit tests in all units of a microservice.

According to Robert V. Head, in his book *Real-Time Business Systems*, the programmer who writes the code should perform the unit testing, because of their knowledge of every niche of the program. They can easily access all the different parts of the program, and hence, make the testing process very easy to execute, while also saving a lot of time.

Unit testing can be used for many different applications. Here are some details of these other uses:

- **Test-driven development**: In this process, tests are written before any code that is to be tested. Based on the tests, programs are then written that are able to pass the test cases for further usage.

- **Work check**: While test-driven development is a nice concept, it is not everyone's cup of tea. The unit testing is about to test our written codes and make corrections to them.

- **Code documentation**: Documentation is a strenuous task, and takes a lot of work to prepare, because of the continuous changes that are made to the code. Unit testing helps documentation by providing pieces of code that explain the product.

Unit testing alone doesn't determine the behavior of the system. Unit tests have good coverage of each of the core modules of the system in isolation. To verify that each module correctly interacts with its collaborators, more coarse-grained testing is required.

# Unit testing – an example

Let's look at an example and build a unit test for a controller class of an ACCOUNT-SERVICE. We will take a simplified version of the `AccountController` class with a single method, as demonstrated here:

```
@RestController
public class AccountController {
        @Autowired
        AccountRepository accountRepository;
        public AccountController(AccountRepository accountRepository) {
                super();
                this.accountRepository = accountRepository;
        }
        ...
        @GetMapping(value = "/account/{accountId}")
        public Account findByAccountId (@PathVariable Integer
accountId){
                return
accountRepository.findAccountByAccountId(accountId);
        }
        ...
}
```

The preceding class has many methods, but in this chapter I will unit-test the findByAccountId(accountId) method, which could look like this:

```
package com.dineshonjava.bookshop.accountservice;
import static org.hamcrest.core.Is.is;
import static org.junit.Assert.assertThat;
import static org.mockito.BDDMockito.given;
import static org.mockito.MockitoAnnotations.initMocks;
import org.junit.Before;
import org.junit.Test;
import org.mockito.Mock;
import
com.dineshonjava.bookshop.accountservice.controller.AccountController;
import com.dineshonjava.bookshop.accountservice.domain.Account;
import
com.dineshonjava.bookshop.accountservice.repository.AccountRepository;
public class AccountControllerTest {
          AccountController accountController;
          @Mock
          AccountRepository accountRepository;
          @Before
          public void setUp() throws Exception {
                    initMocks(this);
                    accountController = new
                    AccountController(accountRepository);
          }
          @Test
          public void findByAccountId (){
                    Account account = new Account();
given(accountRepository.findAccountByAccountId(1000)).willReturn(account);
                    Account acct =
                    accountController.findByAccountId(1002);
                    assertThat(acct.getName(), is("Arnav Rajput"));
          }
}
```

In the preceding test, the class has a `test` method that uses `junit`. We have used `Mockito` to replace the real `AccountRepository` class with a stub object. A stub object is a fake object—stubbing makes our unit testing simple. In the preceding `test` class, we have one `test` method for the `findByAccountId()` method. This `test` method tests the `findByAccountId()` method of the `AccountController` class.

In this application, we use the Spring Boot test library by adding the following Maven dependency:

```
<dependency>
        <groupId>org.springframework.boot</groupId>
        <artifactId>spring-boot-starter-test</artifactId>
        <scope>test</scope>
</dependency>
```

The preceding Maven dependency adds a Spring testing module to your application.

# Integration testing

An integration test is the opposite of a unit test. In the microservice architecture, integration testing is typically used to verify interactions between different layers of integration code and external components such as database and external REST APIs. Integration test can be used to test other microservices, including data stores and caches.

Each microservice must be verified and tested individually, with well-performed unit test cases. However, each microservice communicates with other microservices, so the proper functioning of inter-service communications is a very critical part of microservice architecture testing. Microservice calls must be made successfully with integration with external services.

Microservice integration testing validates that the distributed system is working together with external dependencies smoothly, and also checks that all external or internal dependencies between the services are present as expected. See the following diagram on integration testing:

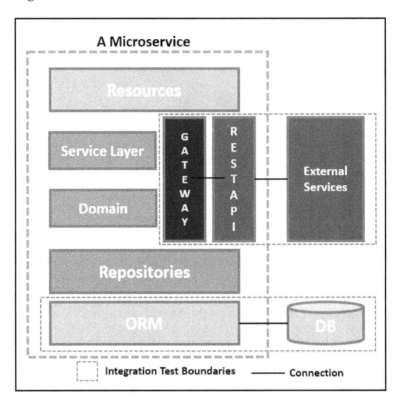

In the preceding diagram, which looks at integration-testing a microservice, we test external dependencies, such as external services and external databases. In this diagram, we implement integration tests for gateway and persistence integration. The gateway integration test ensures that any protocol-related functionality is working properly, and also tests for protocol errors, such as missing HTTP headers, incorrect SSL handling, and so on.

The persistence integration test allows you to test database level errors, such as schema mismatches and mapping issues, as well as ORM tool compatibility.

In integration testing, different units of code are combined together in the form of a group and then tested. Through integration testing, we are able to recognize any errors in the interactions of different units with each other and/or the interface. In the case of small-scale software, integration testing can be done in a single step. However, for big software applications, integration testing is done in different phases. In this case, it can then take various steps. These phases may include the integration of modules into low-level subsystems, preparing them to be integrated into larger subsystems, and eventually completing the software. With integration testing, you can check all aspects of the software, such as its performance, functionality, and reliability.

While unit testing consists of testing different units of the code to isolate any errors in the system, integration testing comprises testing the system in little groups, made up of units, to check their interactions with each other, as well as the functionality of the whole code.

With integration testing, the following three kinds of strategy are commonly used:

- **Big bang**: With this strategy, modules are integrated into a process through which the whole software system is built. This is a high-risk approach because, to deploy it successfully, complete and accurate documentation is required. Otherwise, even the slightest mistakes could cause the whole system to fail.

- **Bottom-up**: With the bottom-up technique, testing starts at the bottom of the hierarchy with the low-level components. Building up from there, the testing continues to the top-level components, until all components are fully tested. Through this strategy, errors can be detected efficiently.

- **Top-down**: With the top-down strategy, top-level integrated modules are tested first, and subsystems are then tested individually. This way, any missing links can be detected easily.

We have previously discussed unit and integration testing for microservice-based applications. Unit testing alone doesn't provide a sufficient output for the behavior of the distributed system, so we need to use integration testing as well. We also need some other approach to testing for microservices. Let's discuss component-testing a microservice-based application in the next section.

# Database integration testing – an example

Let's take a look at an example of a database integration test for `AccountRepository`. This is a repository class for the Account entity in the code base. We will write a unit to test its `findAccountById()` method implementation. Consider the following integration testing class for the `AccountRepository`:

```
package com.dineshonjava.bookshop.accountservice;

import static org.hamcrest.core.Is.is;
import static org.junit.Assert.assertThat;


import org.junit.After;
import org.junit.Test;
import org.junit.runner.RunWith;
import org.springframework.beans.factory.annotation.Autowired;
import org.springframework.boot.test.autoconfigure.orm.jpa.DataJpaTest;
import org.springframework.test.context.junit4.SpringRunner;


import com.dineshonjava.bookshop.accountservice.domain.Account;
import
com.dineshonjava.bookshop.accountservice.repository.AccountRepository;


@RunWith(SpringRunner.class)
@DataJpaTest
public class AccountRepositoryIntegrationTest {
        @Autowired
        private AccountRepository accountRepository;
        @After
        public void tearDown() throws Exception {
                accountRepository.deleteAll();
        }
@Test
        public void shouldSaveAndFetchAccount() throws Exception {
                Account accountA = new Account(1002, "Arnav
Rajput", "Noida", "9431XXX133", "arnav.mail@my.com");
                accountRepository.save(accountA);
                Account accountB =
accountRepository.findAccountByAccountId(1002);
                assertThat(accountB, is(accountA));
        }
}
```

As you can see in the preceding integration class, we have written an integration test to test a database by saving and fetching the `account` object. In integration testing, we can test the integration of the database and other services. In the next section, we'll take a look at how to write an integration test for the REST API call.

# REST API integration – an example

Spring MVC provides an integration testing utility named `MockMvc`. We can use this to write an integration test for REST API controller classes. Let's see how this works for the `/account/<accountId>` endpoint of the `AccountController` class:

```
package com.dineshonjava.bookshop.accountservice;
import static org.mockito.BDDMockito.given;
import static
org.springframework.test.web.servlet.request.MockMvcRequestBuilders.get;
import static
org.springframework.test.web.servlet.result.MockMvcResultMatchers.content;
import static
org.springframework.test.web.servlet.result.MockMvcResultMatchers.status;
import org.junit.Test;
import org.junit.runner.RunWith;
import org.springframework.beans.factory.annotation.Autowired;
import org.springframework.boot.test.autoconfigure.web.servlet.WebMvcTest;
import org.springframework.boot.test.mock.mockito.MockBean;
import org.springframework.test.context.junit4.SpringRunner;
import org.springframework.test.web.servlet.MockMvc;
import
com.dineshonjava.bookshop.accountservice.controller.AccountController;
import com.dineshonjava.bookshop.accountservice.domain.Account;
import
com.dineshonjava.bookshop.accountservice.repository.AccountRepository;

@RunWith(SpringRunner.class)
@WebMvcTest(controllers = AccountController.class)
public class AccountControllerIntegrationTest {
        @Autowired
        private MockMvc mockMvc;
        @MockBean
        private AccountRepository accountRepository;
        @Test
        public void shouldReturnFullName() throws Exception {
                Account rushika = new Account(1003, "Rushika
Rajput", "Noida", "9832XXX23", "rushika.raj@mail.com");
given(accountRepository.findAccountByAccountId(10003)).willReturn(rushika);
                mockMvc.perform(get("/account/10003"))
```

```
                                .andExpect(content().string("Hello Rushika
   Rajput!"))
                                .andExpect(status().is2xxSuccessful());
            }
   }
```

In the preceding integration `test` class, we defined a `test` method for the `findAccountById()` method of the `AccountController` class by using the `MockMvc` framework. In the preceding class, we used the `@WebMvcTest` annotation to tell Spring which controller we're testing. We also used the `@MockBean` annotation to mock the `AccountRepository` class in our Spring context.

# Component testing

Once we have done unit and integration testing for all functions of the modules within a microservice, we need to test each microservice in isolation. A distributed system might be composed of a number of microservices. So, when it comes to testing a microservice in isolation, we have to create a mock of other microservices. Consider the following diagram on component-testing a microservice:

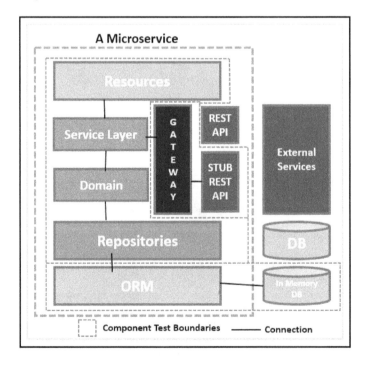

Component testing involves testing the interaction of a microservice with its dependencies, such as a database, all as one unit.

Component testing tests the separation of a component from a large system. A component is a well defined and encapsulated part of a large system, which can be independently replaced. Consequently, testing such components in an isolated system provides many benefits, such as the separation of concern among components of the application, as well as also testing the complexity of a microservice with external services. So, external services and external data stores must be replaceable with stub services and in-memory data stores respectively.

# Contract testing

Contract testing is all about testing the contract between the consumer and producer services. Consider the following diagram showing contract testing:

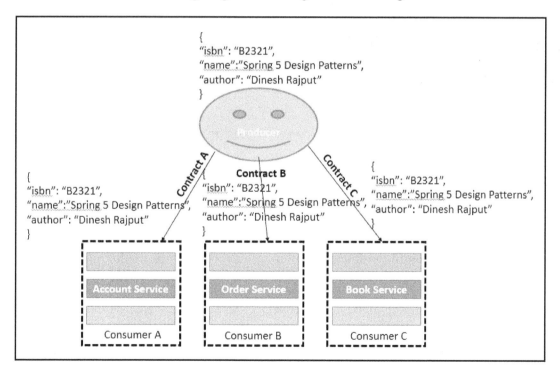

As you can see in this diagram, each consumer has a particular contract with the producer. This contract is about the expected structure of input and output data between the producer and consumer services. Each consumer service has a different contract with the producer service, as per as its requirements. If services change over time, then contracts between the services must be satisfied.

Contract testing tests the input and output of service calls that contain certain attributes and also tests throughput latency. Contract testing is not a component test; it doesn't test the component deeply, but rather, it only tests the data structure with the required attributes for the input and output of service calls.

In the preceding diagram, suppose that a producer service exposes a resource with three attributes: ISBN, name, and author. This resource represents book information that is then adopted by three different consumer services.

# End-to-end testing

With end-to-end testing, an application is tested to check whether or not it has a complete flow from the beginning to the end. Through end-to-end testing, any system dependencies are weeded out and integrity between different components is maintained. Here, the intention is to verify that the system as a whole meets business goals, irrespective of the component architecture in use.

In a microservice-based application, end-to-end testing provides value by covering the gaps between the services.

End-to-end testing checks all the critical functionalities for any bugs or anomalies, such as communication within or outside of the system, the application's interface, the database, network, and other components. There are two different ways of performing end-to-end testing:

- **Horizontal end-to-end testing**: This is the more common method for implementing end-to-end testing. In horizontal testing, the test adopts a user's perspective and then navigates through the whole system. If any anomalies or bugs are found, then they are reported; otherwise, the system works exactly as it should.

- **Vertical end-to-end testing**: With this method, the testing is done in a hierarchical order. Here, all the components of the system are checked individually and thoroughly to ensure the quality of the complete code. This testing process is not as popular as horizontal end-to-end testing, as it is mostly only used for complex computing program testing.

To understand the different types of end-to-end testing on an application, take the example of an e-commerce web application. With a horizontal end-to-end test, the process will be to sign in, check the profile, use the search bar, add an item to a cart, save any item to be bought later, check out, add payment information, confirm the purchase, and sign out. However, a vertical end-to-end testing method is more likely to be used by a program without any user interface, or perhaps a more complex application than that of a simple e-commerce website. Let's consider the following diagram showing the end-to-end testing of a microservice-based application:

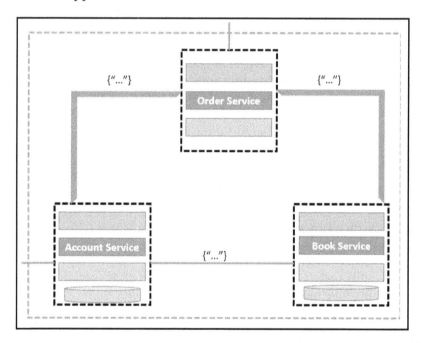

As you can see in the preceding diagram, each service communicates with other microservices with some contract of input and output data structure.

We can use Selenium and WebDriver protocol tools for the end-to-end testing of a microservice-based application. Selenium needs a browser, and it can use that browser for tests. Let's add the Firefox driver with Selenium by adding the following Maven dependency:

```
<dependency>
    <groupId>org.seleniumhq.selenium</groupId>
    <artifactId>selenium-firefox-driver</artifactId>
    <version>3.14.0</version>
</dependency>
```

The Selenium Firefox dependency is suitable for a web application when UI/functional testing is required. Let's discuss UI/functional testing in the next section.

# UI/functional testing

In functional testing, each and every aspect of code is tested to make sure that it is working correctly. In simple terms, functional testing considers the system's requirements and checks whether the system is fulfilling them. Anything that is done differently, or not done at all, will be listed as an anomaly. Consequently, functional testing is essential for looking at code execution and making sure that it is done right.

When performing functional testing, the process is as follows:

1. First, data is input
2. Next, it is determined what the output is supposed to be
3. The test is then run with the relevant input
4. Finally, the output results are compared with the expected results

In the end, if the results match, then it is clear that the system is working perfectly, but if they are different, then this means that bugs have been found.

In UI testing, the system is checked for bugs and anomalies with the help of a **graphical user interface** (**GUI**). UI testing is done in a hierarchical order, moving from tester's frontend issues to backend issues, and checking everything along the way.

UI testing can be done accurately with the help of the following approaches:

- **Manual-based testing**: This approach is based on the knowledge about the domain and the application. Unless the tester knows what to test, it cannot be executed properly.

- **Capture and replay**: This method depends on having a user go through the system and capture all activity. All of these activities are then replayed to make sure that the user did not face any anomalies in the system.

- **Model-based testing**: In this method, all the events of the GUI are executed at least once.

In this chapter, we have discussed most testing strategies. However, how to write tests for a particular microservice depends on its business boundaries.

# Summary

In this chapter, we have discussed testing strategies for a microservice. Testing a microservice requires a high level of confidence in it. In the microservice architecture, an application has many more moving parts in comparison to others.

Unit testing tests the smallest piece of a microservice to determine if its behavior is as expected. Integration testing tests external dependencies and their communication methods between components, either externally or internally. Component testing verifies a microservice behavior in isolation from any external dependencies, whereas contract testing tests interactions at the boundary of an external service. End-to-end testing verifies the whole system, and this should ultimately meet the expected business goal.

In `Chapter 8`, *Performance Testing of Microservices*, we'll discuss the microservice approach to designing performance testing, and we'll also look at load testing tools for microservice testing, including Jmeter, the Ready API, and Gatling.

# 8
# Performance Testing of Microservices

In the previous chapter, we discussed how to carry out functional testing of a microservice to ensure the quality of the intended requirement. We have written unit tests to ensure that individual units function as expected and integration tests to check external dependencies, such as databases or external service calls. However, in a microservice-based architecture, performance testing is needed to test all individual components, such as the microservices themselves, the REST API, or the database. Performance testing ensures the performance of the overall application, allowing it to send fast responses to clients.

When designing a performance test for a microservice-based application, it has to test the performance of the APIs as well as the performance of external dependencies. Load testing tools such as JMeter, the Ready API, or Gatling can be used to design scripts to test microservices.

After completing this chapter, the reader will be able to design a strategy for performance testing microservices by studying successful use cases. I will demonstrate how to test microservices using tools such as JMeter and Gatling.

This chapter will cover the following topics:

- JMeter
- Installing JMeter
- Performance testing microservices with JMeter
- Gatling
- Installing Gatling
- Performance testing microservices with Gatling
- The ReadyAPI

Let's take a look at these topics in detail.

# Technical Requirements

You will be required to have Spring Boot 2.0, Java 8, Spring Tool Suite Version 3.9.5 release, Maven, and JMeter installed to follow the procedure.

The code files of this chapter can be found on GitHub:
`https://github.com/PacktPublishing/Hands-On-Microservices-Monitoring-and-Testing/tree/master/Chapter08`

Check out the following video to see the code in action:
`http://bit.ly/2yzoRmw`

# JMeter

JMeter was first developed by Stefano Mazzochi from Apache software. It was originally designed for the purpose of testing the **Apache JServ Protocol** (**AJP**) but was redesigned by Apache with an enhanced GUI and the ability to perform functional testing. It is now an open-source testing software that is made up of pure Java applications for the purpose of load and performance testing. It covers a wide variety of test categories, including functional, load, performance, and regression.

The protocols that JMeter supports include the following:

- The web, including HTTP and HTTPS sites
- Web services, such as SOAP/XML-RPC
- Databases via JDBC drivers
- Directories, such as LDAP
- Messaging-oriented services via JMS
- Services, such as POP3, IMAP, and SMTP
- FTP services

With a simple GUI, JMeter can conduct load and performance tests and is completely platform-free, whether you are running it on Linux or Windows. In the following section, we'll learn how to install JMeter on your machine.

# Installing JMeter

To install JMeter on your machine, regardless of whether you are using Windows or Linux, follow these steps:

1. Install Java Check, regardless of whether you have Java installed. JMeter is a Java-based desktop application, so it requires Java to be installed. You need to install Java 8+ to get the latest version of JMeter.
2. Download JMeter after installing Java on your machine. You can download the latest version of JMeter from `http://jmeter.apache.org/download_jmeter.cgi`. There are two binary files here in the `.zip` and `.tgz` formats. You can choose either, depending on your machine. For JMeter 4.0, the system must have Java 8 or 9 installed.
3. JMeter is very easy to install. You simply unzip the downloaded file. JMeter has numerous directories and important files.
4. Launch JMeter. If you are using a Windows machine, go to `apache-jmeter-4.0\bin` and run the `jmeter.bat` file.

You can also launch JMeter in non-GUI mode by running the bat file `bin\jmeter-server.bat`. This can be done by using the following command:

```
$jmeter -n -t testPlan.jmx - l log.jtl -H 127.0.0.1 -P 8000
```

The elements of this command are as follows:

- `jmeter -n`: This specifies that JMeter is to run in command-line mode
- `-t ttestPlan.jmx`: This indicates that the name of the file contains a test plan
- `-l log.jtl`: This indicates that the log file stores the test result
- `-H 127.0.0.1 -P 8000`: The server's hostname and port

In the next section, we will discuss how to carry out performance testing of a microservice-based application using JMeter.

# Performance testing microservices with JMeter

JMeter can be used to performance-test your microservice applications. It includes the following tests:

- **Load test**: Multiple users can access the microservice concurrently to test its expected usage.
- **Stress test**: This tests the maximum load capacity. The purpose of stress testing is to recognize the maximum load that the server can handle without any errors.

JMeter creates a copy of the samplers, which can then be run in multiple threads. The following diagram shows how JMeter's load test simulates a heavy load:

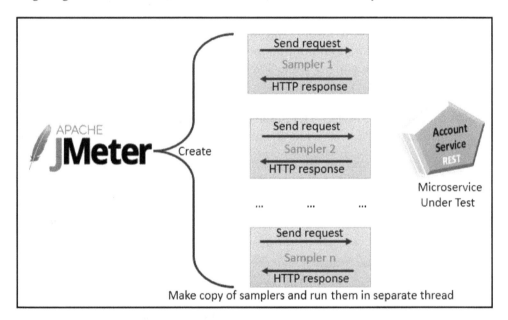

In the preceding diagram, you can see that there are a number of samplers for the microservice that is being tested. We'll now look at how to create performance test plans.

# Creating a performance test plan

Let's imagine that we are carrying out a performance analysis of the account service for 1,000 users. Follow these steps to learn how to create a performance test plan for a microservice:

1. **Adding a thread group**: Start by creating a thread group. Start JMeter, select the test plan, and add a thread group, as follows:

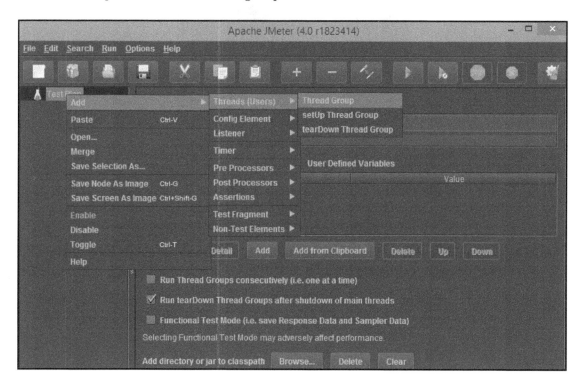

As you can see in the preceding screenshot, this is done by right-clicking on **Test Plan** and then selecting **Add | Threads (Users) | Thread Group.** Let's add this thread information to the thread group, as follows:

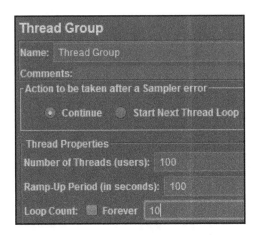

In the preceding screenshot, we have added **100** threads, which is the number of users who will connect to the targeted microservice. Those **100** users connect to the microservice **10** times each. We have also provided a **100** second ramp-up time period for the **100** users, which equates to one per user, per second.

2. **Configuring JMeter elements**: Let's configure JMeter's elements for this thread group. JMeter's elements are what you want to test.

   First, we are going to configure HTTP Request Defaults. Right-click on **Thread Group** and select **Add | Config Element | HTTP Request Defaults**, as shown in the following screenshot:

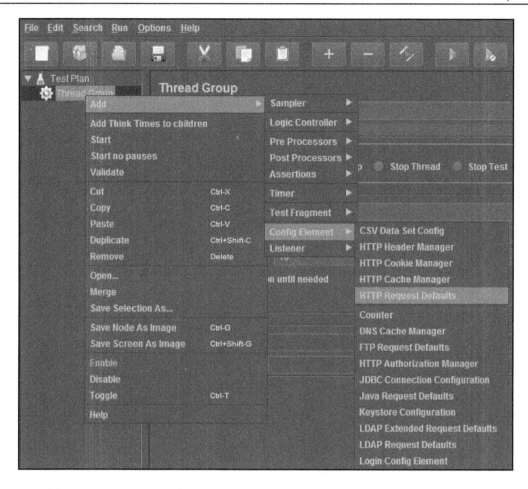

Here, we can enter information about our microservice in the **HTTP Request Defaults** control panel. Let's suppose our microservice is hosted on `www.dineshonjava.com`. This is shown in the following screenshot:

You can also add other JMeter elements to this thread group, such as HTTP Request. Right-click on **Thread Group** and select **Add** ǀ **Sampler** ǀ **HTTP Request**. Then, add the element information to the control panel.

3. **Adding a report element**: Right-click on **Test Plan** and select **Add** ǀ **Listener** ǀ **Graph Results**, as shown in the following screenshot:

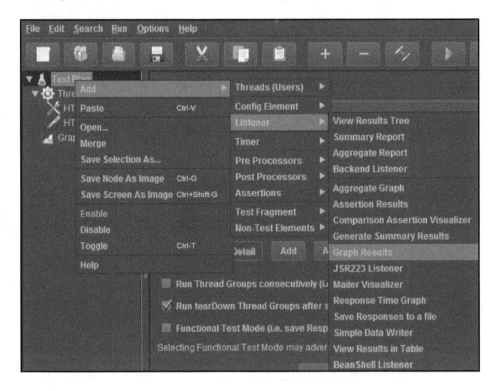

As you can see in the preceding screenshot, clicking on this option will show the test results in graph format.

4. **Running the performance test**: You can run the performance test by using the keyboard command *Ctrl + R* or by using the **Run** button on JMeter's toolbar. You will see the test result displayed in graph format in real time. This is shown in the following screenshot:

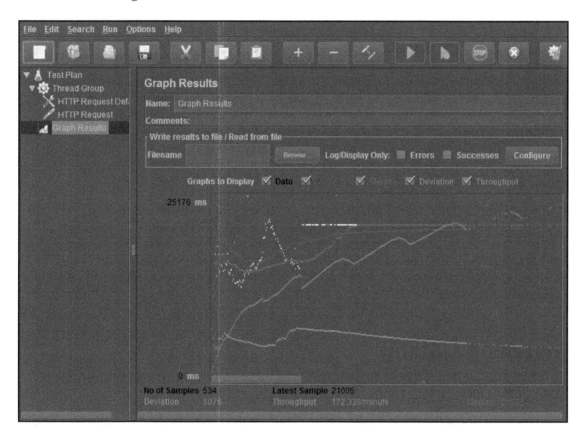

The preceding graph contains the following performance statistics about the targeted website and the microservice:

- The number of samples sent to the website
- The average of the all samples sent
- The deviation for the samples
- The throughput rate, which represents the number of requests per minute handled by the server

In this section, we have looked at how to carry out performance testing of a microservice with JMeter and how to configure different JMeter elements and report formats as per your requirements. We'll look at another tool for carrying out performance testing in the next section.

# Gatling

Gatling is an open-source platform that was established for the purpose of testing load and performance. This software implements load testing over an application, meaning that you can determine the performance of various services while still focusing on the web application. With Gatling, you can create your own tests by using the Scala programming language. Although this language is not very well-known, tests that are developed with it are. Gatling has become quite popular over the last couple of years and is used by a significant number of developers and testers.

Gatling also provides a detailed dashboard that shows you the results of the tests that you have performed. Without making use of any added plugins, the system also generates a report of the results in HTML format. This report can be easily saved on the device for further use and analysis, or for metric comparisons with other tests. The report is also interactive, which means that you can zoom in to specific areas of the report and perform a more detailed analysis.

# Installing Gatling

To install Gatling on your machine, regardless of whether you are using Windows or Linux, follow these steps:

1. Install Java. Gatling requires that Java 8+ is installed on your machine. You have to install Java 8+ to be able to get the latest version of Gatling.
2. Download Gatling. Go to Gatling's official website (`https://gatling.io/download/`) and download the latest version of Gatling.
3. Install Gatling. Gatling is easy to install. Simply unzip the downloaded file. Gatling has numerous directories and important files.

4. Set the system properties. If you are using the Windows system, go to the system properties and set the environment variables `GATLING_HOME` and Path:
`GATLING_HOME=D:/gatling-charts-highcharts-bundle-2.3.1`
`Path= %GATLING_HOME%\bin`.

5. Finally, launch Gatling. If you are using a Windows machine, go to `gatling-charts-highcharts-bundle-2.3.1\bin` and run the `gatling.bat` file.

We have successfully launched the Gatling testing tool. In the next section, we'll look at how to do performance testing with Gatling.

# Performance testing with Gatling

Load testing a microservice-based application is an important practice. As a developer, you can choose any one of the many popular, open source load testing tools. In this section, I am going to explain the Gatling load testing tool.

In the previous section, we discussed Apache JMeter. Apache JMeter is a very powerful load testing tool, but Gatling provides another advantage to developers, which is the Scala development language for test creation.

Let's test one of the application's microservice using Gatling. We will use a microservice that has been built using Java and Spring Boot. If you have already installed Gatling, check which version you have and make sure that it's the latest version. Perform following steps to carry out a load test with Gatling:

1. **Adding a build dependency for the Gatling API tool**:

   **In Maven**:

   Add the following dependency in the `pom.xml` file:

```
<dependency>
        <groupId>io.gatling.highcharts</groupId>
        <artifactId>gatling-charts-highcharts</artifactId>
        <version>2.3.1</version>
</dependency>
```

**In Gradle**:

Add the following dependency in the `build.gradle` file:

```
{
apply plugin: 'scala'
...
testCompile group: 'io.gatling.highcharts', name: 'gatling-
charts-highcharts', version: '2.3.1'
...
}
```

Next, we'll look at how to carry out a load test on a microservice.

2. **Microservices under load testing**: Take a look at the following REST endpoints. These are the ones that we want to load-test using Gatling:

```
@RestController
public class AccountController {
        @Autowired
        AccountRepository accountRepository;
        ...
        @PostMapping(value = "/account")
        public Account save (@RequestBody Account account){
                return accountRepository.save(account);
        }
        @GetMapping(value = "/account/{accountId}")
        public Account findByAccountId (@PathVariable Integer
accountId){
                return
accountRepository.findAccountByAccountId(accountId);
        }
        ...
}
```

Tests for two endpoints (`/account` and `/account/{accountId}`), as shown in the preceding code snippet. Let's move on to the next step, where we will show you how to write tests for the preceding two endpoints using Scala.

3. **Writing a simulation file and providing test scenarios**: Create a `scala` project and write a `scala` class, `AccountGatlingSimulation.scala`, for the Account Service. Take a look at the following `scala` file for load testing:

```scala
package dineshonjava
import io.gatling.core.Predef._
import io.gatling.http.Predef._
import scala.concurrent.duration._
class AccountGatlingSimulation extends Simulation{
        val scn = scenario("AddAndFindAccount").repeat(500,
          "n") {
        exec(
        http("AddAccount-API")
          .post("http://localhost:1111/account")
          .header("Content-Type", "application/json")
          .body(StringBody("""{"accountId":${n},
        "name":"Arnav${n}","email":"arnav${n}@mail.com",
        "mobile":"9334343${n}
        ","address": "Noida:${n}"}"""))
          .check(status.is(200))
        ).pause(2)
        }.repeat(500, "n") {
        exec(
          http("GetAccount-API")
            .get("http://localhost:1111/account/${n}")
            .check(status.is(200))
        )
    }
  setUp(scn.inject(atOnceUsers(30))).maxDuration(
   FiniteDuration.apply(5, "minutes"))
  }
```

As you can see, in the Gatling test suite this class is written in `scala`, and every Gatling test class should extend a simulation class. You can define several Gatling test suits inside this class using Gatling's Scala **Domain-Specific Language** (**DSL**).

In the preceding Gatling test suite class, we will run 30 threads or clients that will send parallel requests 500 times each. In the first test suite, the threads add a new account to the database by using a REST endpoint, that is, the POST /account method. In the second test suite, the threads search the account by using another REST endpoint, the GET /account/{accountId} method. In total, this means that the threads will send 30,000 requests to the Account Service: 15,000 to the POST endpoint, and 15,000 to the GET endpoint. Let's move on and look at how we can run this test class.

4. **Running Gatling tests**: You can run a Gatling test in one of two ways: by adding the Maven plugin, or by adding the Gradle plugin and the Gatling GUI tools. In the next section, we'll look at the first of these approaches.

# Maven plugin configuration

There are some Maven plugins available that provide support for running tests while building a project. Take a look at the following Maven plugin setup configuration:

```
<plugin>
  <groupId>io.gatling</groupId>
  <artifactId>gatling-maven-plugin</artifactId>
  <version>2.3.1</version>
  <!-- optional if you only have one simulation -->
  <configuration>
<simulationClass>dineshonjava.AccountGatlingSimulation</simulationClass>
<configFolder>${project.basedir}/src/test/resources</configFolder>
<dataFolder>${project.basedir}/src/test/resources/data</dataFolder>
<resultsFolder>${project.basedir}/target/gatling/results</resultsFolder>
<bodiesFolder>${project.basedir}/src/test/resources/bodies</bodiesFolder>
<simulationsFolder>${project.basedir}/src/test/scala</simulationsFolder>
            <runDescription>This Account Microservice Gatling Performance
test for a Microservice</runDescription>
  </configuration>
    <executions>
      <execution>
        <goals>
          <goal>integration-test</goal>
        </goals>
      </execution>
    </executions>
</plugin>
```

As you can see in the preceding configuration, we have set up the Maven plugin for Gatling to run load testing. The preceding configuration must be added if you want to run a Gatling test via the following command:

```
mvn gatling:test
```

# Gradle plugin configuration

There are some Gradle plugins available that provide support for running tests during the build of a project. However, we can also define a simple Gradle task that just runs tests by using the `io.gatling.app.Gatling` class:

```
task loadTest(type: JavaExec) {
    dependsOn testClasses
    description = "This Account Microservice Gatling Performance test
    for a Microservice."
    group = "Load Test"
    classpath = sourceSets.test.runtimeClasspath
    jvmArgs = [
        "-
Dgatling.core.directory.binaries=${sourceSets.test.output.classesDir.toStri
ng()}"
    ]
    main = "io.gatling.app.Gatling"
    args = [
        "--simulation", "dineshonjava.AccountGatlingSimulation",
        "--results-folder", "${buildDir}/gatling-results",
        "--binaries-folder",
      sourceSets.test.output.classesDir.toString(),
        "--bodies-folder",
      sourceSets.test.resources.srcDirs.toList().first().toString() +
      "/gatling/bodies",
    ]
}
```

The preceding code must be added to a `build.gradle` file. This is the default way of creating custom tasks for Gradle. It is a *JavaExec* type task, with test class dependencies. This means that it has nothing to do with the main classes.

In the preceding configuration, the most important thing is the `args` attribute values, where we let Gatling know about the *simulation* to be executed, the *result-folder* to be used to store reports, and the *bodies-folder* to be used to get body files. These body files are for requests that require a body.

# Running a Gatling test suite using the Gatling GUI

Let's take a look at how to run Gatling test suites by using the Gatling GUI. Start the Gatling GUI by double-clicking on the `recorder.bat` file on Windows or the `recorder.sh` file on Linux. Set up the configuration for the target simulation, as follows:

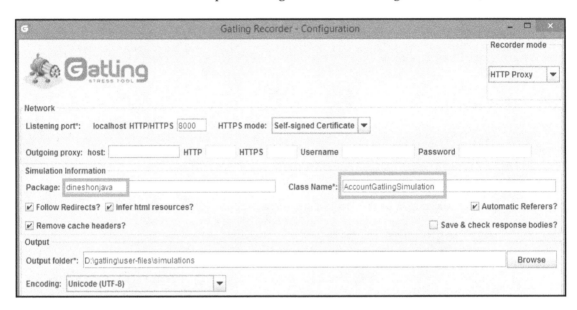

As you can see in the preceding screenshot, we have added the package name and the class name. Click on the **Start** button and run the Gatling tool by double-clicking the `gatling.bat` file on Windows or the `gatling.sh` file on Linux. After starting Gatling, it will look something like the following:

```
GATLING_HOME is set to "D:\gatling"
JAVA = """C:\Program Files\Java\jdk1.8.0_121\bin\java.exe"""
Choose a simulation number:
     [0] computerdatabase.BasicSimulation
     [1] computerdatabase.advanced.AdvancedSimulationStep01
     [2] computerdatabase.advanced.AdvancedSimulationStep02
     [3] computerdatabase.advanced.AdvancedSimulationStep03
     [4] computerdatabase.advanced.AdvancedSimulationStep04
     [5] computerdatabase.advanced.AdvancedSimulationStep05
     [6] dineshonjava.AccountGatlingSimulation
     [7] dineshonjava.ApiGatlingSimulationTest
6
Select simulation id (default is 'accountgatlingsimulation'). Accepted character
s are a-z, A-Z, 0-9, - and _
```

In the preceding screenshot, Gatling is asking us to select a simulation class for all of the available simulations. We have selected **6** for the `dineshonjava.AccountGatlingSimulation` class. You can also add a simulation ID and simulation description, but these are optional fields. Press the *Enter* button in the console; you will receive the following output:

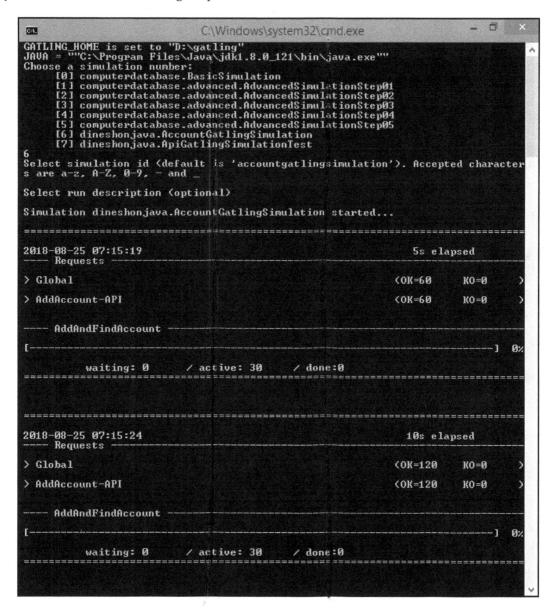

As you can see in the preceding screenshot, the test suites are running and printing logs in the console. They will start adding accounts into the database that contain all of the active users; these are the 30 clients we talked about previously.

After a while, the test will finish and print the following report to the console:

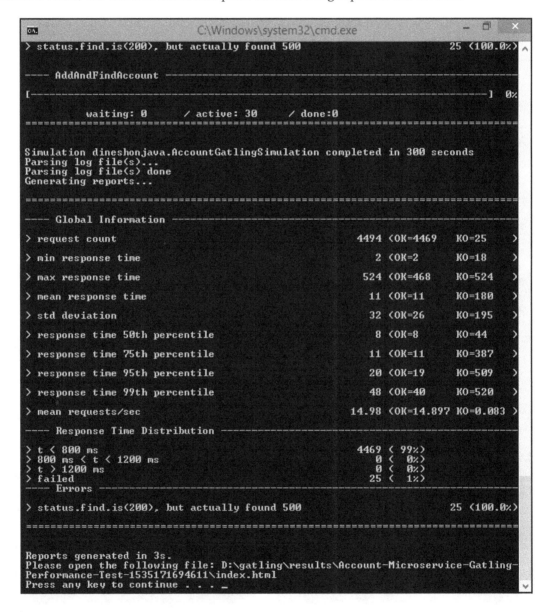

As you can see in the preceding screenshot, the load testing reports for the application are displayed in the console, which we will look at further in the following step.

After load testing has finished, Gatling will have generated the report in a particular location. In our case, the generated report will be saved to this location: `D:\gatling\results\Account-Microservice-Gatling-Performance-Test-1535171694611`. This is shown in the following screenshot:

| Local Disk (D:) ▸ gatling ▸ results ▸ Account-Microservice-Gatling-Performance-Test-1535171694611 | | | |
|---|---|---|---|
| Name | Date modified | Type | Size |
| js | Sat 25-Aug-2018 1... | File folder | |
| style | Sat 25-Aug-2018 1... | File folder | |
| index.html | Sat 25-Aug-2018 1... | Firefox HTML Doc... | 57 KB |
| req_addaccount-api-4807f.html | Sat 25-Aug-2018 1... | Firefox HTML Doc... | 50 KB |
| simulation.log | Sat 25-Aug-2018 1... | Text Document | 349 KB |

In the preceding screenshot, the index file of the generated report is `index.html`. If you open this file, you'll be able to view more details, as follows:

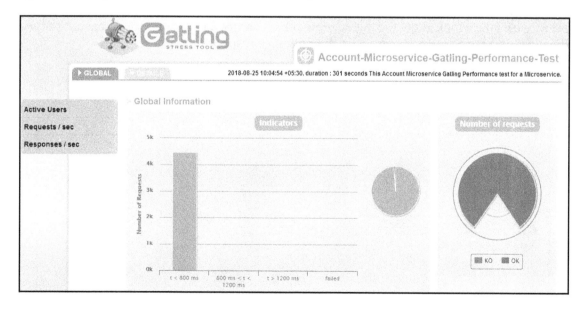

We can choose to look at a report for all requests or filter them to see only those that are generated by a selected API. In the following screenshot, we can see a report just for `AddAccount-API`:

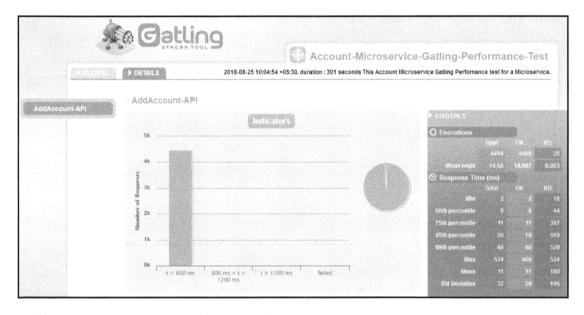

Now, we'll take a look at the format of a few other reports. The following screenshot shows the percentage of requests grouped by their average response time:

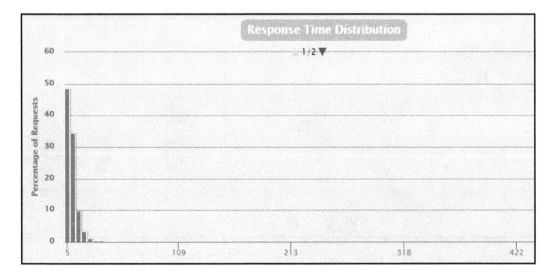

The following screenshot shows a graph that illustrates a timeline with the average response times. It also shows statistics by percentiles:

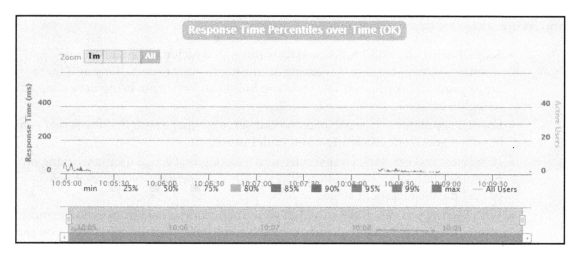

The following graph shows the number of requests that were processed successfully by the application in a second:

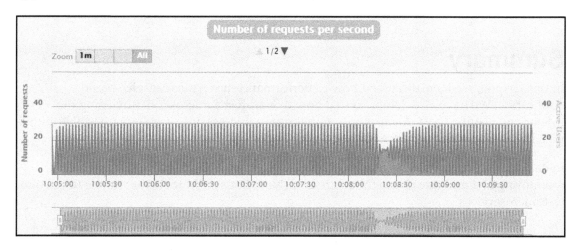

In this section, we have created a Gatling test suite and generated a performance testing report for a microservice. In the next section, we will discuss the Ready API.

# The ReadyAPI

The ReadyAPI is a combination of other services, such as SoapUI Pro, LoadUI Pro, service, and secure. These are explained, as follows:

- SoapUI helps you build functional tests through which you can determine whether your application is working according to your expectations or if there are any anomalies present. The tests you build can vary from being very simple to highly complex.
- LoadUI simulates a massive load on your server to make sure that the server can handle it and work efficiently, even under pressure.
- In Service, you can trick your service into thinking that a real user is working on the application so that you can continue testing the service, even after it has passed the development stage.
- With Secure, you can make sure that your application is safe from even the most common attacks. While it already contains some basic security measures, you can also add a few custom-made security scans for your application.

With the Ready API, you can easily manage your projects and APIs while also implementing customized security measures for your applications.

# Summary

In this chapter, we have discussed how to performance-test a microservice-based application. We have also demonstrated how to load-test a microservice by using the JMeter and Gatling tools. An application that uses a microservice architecture is distributed, which means that performance testing is very important.

In Chapter 9, *Performance Monitoring of Microservices*, we'll discuss the performance monitoring of a microservice architecture and the various APM tools that can be utilized to test microservices.

# 9
# Performance Monitoring of Microservices

In the previous chapter, we discussed how to carry out performance testing for a microservice-based application. Performance or load testing is a critical part of any application that serves a lot of users. A microservice-based application has a lot of small services that run on separate servers, and each microservice can be written in any language. For this reason, it is important that load testing is performed for each microservice.

This chapter will discuss performance monitoring of microservice-based architectures. We will look at various **Application Performance Management** (**APM**) tools that can be utilized to test microservices, and will also learn about performance counters that are specific to microservices.

After reading this chapter, you will be able to diagnose performance issues related to microservices and APIs using monitoring tools. You will also be able to identify performance issues in a microservice by going through production logs and monitoring tools. You will be provided with a list of the most common performance issues related to microservices and will learn how to tune their performance.

This chapter will cover the following topics:

- Identifying performance counters to test microservices
- Performance monitoring tools, such as:
  - AppDynamics
  - Dynatrace
  - AWS CloudWatch
  - Nagios
  - New Relic
  - Datadog (for Docker performance monitoring)

- Component-level monitoring
- Domain-specific monitoring
- Dashboards and identifying issues by going through logs

Let's get started and take a look at these topics in detail.

# Identifying performance counters to test microservices

In the microservice architecture pattern, a distributed system runs on several different machines, where each service is a component or process of an enterprise application. Although using a microservice-based application has a lot of advantages, it can bring about major challenges as well. One such challenge includes how to monitor a distributed system; this is because each microservice is heterogeneous and independent in nature. This means that traditional monitoring approaches are not good enough.

Monitoring is a critical part of a microservice-based system. It involves knowing how to control it and to how make sure that software is reliable, available, and that it performs as expected. This isn't a particularly easy task.

As you may know, traditional APM tools that are suitable for monolithic applications are not suitable for complex distributed applications. However, there are APM tools currently available on the market that can be used to monitor a microservice-based application. We will discuss these tools in the following section.

# Performance monitoring tools

In this section, we will discuss a few APM tools that monitor the performance of a microservice-based application—but remember, it can be very difficult to select the right monitoring tool for a microservice-based application. Services can vary vastly in design and can be hosted within virtualized machines or containers located across a private cloud, public cloud, or even both.

The purpose of a monitoring tool is to provide insights about all microservices in a distributed application. Some of the reasons we monitor microservices include the following:

- We get a view of their performance from an ongoing perspective
- We gain the ability to ensure that any new updates or changes do not break monitors in production
- We get a clear insight into the microservices, including their health status, memory, resource utilization, CPU load, disk usage, the number of errors, and so on

There are several APM tools available on the market, so let's get on and have a look at them.

# AppDynamics

AppDynamics is a company based in San Francisco that focuses on APM and operation analytics. The company provides APM tools to developers and architects to sort out performance-related issues. Developers can combine these APM tools with their own analytic approach. AppDynamics provides people with a significant amount of detail, enabling them to solve problems.

The tools provided by AppDynamics baseline-monitor an application's performance and provide reports on issues relating to the performance of an app. AppDynamics, therefore, requires access to all information regarding transactions that are performed in an application.

APM tools are basically designed to cater to production environments that allow for quick and efficient access to crucial transaction details. They are set to automatically detect normal performance behavior and prevent any false alarms, which can be dealt with by dynamic baselining.

AppDynamics keeps track of all transactions by comparing the self-learned baseline and the authentic response time. When any kind of deviation in the usual behavior of a business transaction occurs, the agent gathers all of the call stack's data so that it can help in sorting out possible issues which may have occurred.

This smart analytical technique helps AppDynamics to determine where the problem is before sending out an alert at the very beginning. This helps to solve problems earlier on, before they get too complex to solve.

AppDynamics has a solution for capturing data throughout the entire system. It provides a feature that allows the user to carry out system-wide data recording and capturing. The ideal for pre-production environments is the developer mode, where a transaction snapshot is used to record requests. Most importantly, when it is accidentally left on, the system will shut down immediately. This feature ensures that the system will not stall when the number of transactions increases or decreases.

# Dynatrace

Dynatrace is an APM company that offers IT-related products to IT departments and owners of digital businesses, both small and large. The company provides performance management software for applications and systems running in the cloud or on-premises. Its software helps to manage an application's performance and maintain its availability to users. It also helps to keep track of user experience. This is done by tracing deep transactions, monitoring apps synthetically, monitoring real users, and monitoring the network.

Dynatrace enables the simplified monitoring and troubleshooting of cloud environments through full automation and AI. Dynatrace helps to provide all possible information that may be required by developers and business stakeholders to help improve the performance of the application. This means that both users and developers benefit from its product. The software helps to drive towards better business outcomes, and therefore increases productivity.

The software uses a proactive approach to optimizing user experience. It also ensures that the performance of an application is optimized across the whole stack; it both enhances and accelerates an application's deployment procedure. Dynatrace's DevOps, which are metric-driven, work easily alongside existing development tools that are being utilized in a system. The software provided by Dynatrace offers browser-to-code level visibility, which is an AI-powered anomaly detection technique that traces transactions in a distributive manner. All of these methods and techniques help people to improve an application's performance while eradicating any bottlenecks so that it does not affect the user experience.

Dynatrace's software also has **Digital Experience Monitoring** (**DEM**), which generates an analytical report that is critical for businesses. The reports generated can help the executive members of a company decide how to bring their business forward and provide an insight into how user experience is affected.

# AWS CloudWatch

Amazon CloudWatch can be useful for developers, system architects, and administrators. It helps them monitor their AWS applications that are in the cloud. CloudWatch is designed to provide metrics automatically on the basis of request counts, CPU usage, and latency. Users can send their own metrics and logs to CloudWatch to be monitored.

The data and reports that are provided by CloudWatch help users monitor the performance of their applications, resource utilization, issues regarding operations, and other possible obstacles, helping organizations resolve possible issues in the system.

CloudWatch is most commonly used with **Elastic Compute Cloud** (**EC2**). It can also monitor the **Amazon Elastic Book Store** (**EBS**) and **Elastic Load Balancers** (**ELBs**). It can also bend its core and primary rules to take in custom data, so it can extend its services. The most common reasons users opt for CloudWatch are because of its simple automatic integration with AWS services, the flexibility it provides, and its ability to scale.

To make it work with EC2, Amazon CloudWatch is configured differently and extended. This allows it to offer two distinct levels of monitoring, which are as follows:

- **Basic monitoring**: This package includes seven pre-selected metrics along with three status check metrics, which are each generated at 5 minute and 1 minute intervals respectively; no extra payment is required
- **Detailed monitoring**: With this, users are given the opportunity to perform checks more frequently as intervals are reduced to 1 minute; this package requires extra payment

Additional AWS services that can be automatically monitored by CloudWatch include the following:

- EBS
- RDS database instances
- SQS Queues
- SNS Topics

# Nagios

The network monitoring tool Nagios, which is now known as **Nagios Core**, is a leading solution for most companies that operate on Linux. Nagios is open-source software that is used to monitor IT infrastructures. It can be used both to monitor networks—including servers, routers, switches, and services—and to send an alert to an administrator when something goes wrong or when something starts working again. It detects errors that may occur in the future and repairs them before users are affected.

An updated version of Nagios, known as **Nagios XI**, allows you to customize and personalize the software with additional specifications. It has a complete web and graphical user interface. It also works with pre-existing installations of Nagios and provides the monitoring of an entire system, protocol, database, application, log, and bandwidth. It is freely available for up to seven hosts with no limitation on services.

Nagios provides monitoring for each and every component of an infrastructure, including network protocols, system metrics, operating systems, and services. Simple dashboards and views save time by providing a central view of an entire process and IT network at a single glance. The interface also provides automated capacity planning through graphs of the entire infrastructure. Another helpful specification is multiple user access, which allows both stakeholders and clients to access the tool easily. Advanced user management also allows every user to view only the data that is relevant to them and that they are authorized to see.

To run this application, you need a 20 GB hard drive with at least 2 GB memory and a dual-core 2.4 GHz CPU. Your operating system must be CentOS or **Red hat Enterprise Linux** (**RHEL**) versions 6 or 7 with MySQL or MariaDB, plus a PostgreSQL database.

Like most things, Nagios gives users opportunities, but it has limitations too. First and foremost, to install or configure Nagios, you need a good understanding of Linux. While most of the Nagios interface is easy to use, not all of its plugins integrate well and they are not all high-quality.

# New Relic

New Relic is a software analysis company that was founded in San Francisco in 2008. New Relic allows software developers and technology companies to keep an eye on the performance and maintenance of their applications. Almost 14,000 companies are registered with New Relic and rely on it for their business endeavors. The data analyzed by New Relic is real-time data, which helps companies predict the performance, problems, and also solutions for their web servers and applications.

New Relic provides the following products:

- **APM**: This provides you with the deepest real data about performance. It shows you bottlenecks in your application, server, or database in the form of charts. It can run in seven programming languages.
- **INFRASTRUCTURE**: This product helps you to gather information about your system properties, including memory, CPU usage, and processing. If there are any critical situations, it will alert you on the New Relic dashboard.
- **BROWSER**: The New Relic browser is one of a kind. It will improve your client reliability and your business productivity by decreasing page loading time and removing errors on the frontend.
- **mAPM**: This product is for mobile users (both Android and iOS). It tracks your mobile applications and manages their performance. You can get data about what is making your app slow down, information about the network carrier, and anything else that may improve your mobile app.
- **SYNTHETICS**: This helps you identify errors in your server before your customer can. You can run a test and remove all obstacles that might affect your business.
- **INSIGHTS**: This feature allows you to visualize and evaluate statistics all on one screen. The metric explorer gathers data from all of the products being used. You can also add any chart into Insights to analyze the performance of an application.

New Relic also provides expert services, in which you can ask experts about your problems. They can also provide advice about how to optimize products.

# Datadog (for Docker performance monitoring)

Docker is a platform on which developers can build and deploy software using containers. It has gained a lot of popularity over the last few years. Docker provides methods that help a developer to build software that is productive; developers can also benefit from Docker's bit-for-bit compatibility between different environments. Docker has now become an important tool for solving the constant flow of deliveries that are common within modern infrastructure. Note that the containers used need to have a new, more refined monitoring approach, so if a developer uses Docker, they should opt for the newest integration available—Datadog.

Although this integration helps you monitor containers, it is easier to run version 4.3.1 of the Datadog agent.

If a developer requires a straightforward way to monitor Docker containers, they should be running a Datadog agent on the host. From here, the agent gains access to the statistics of containers, which allows Docker to be deployed on operating systems of recently running hosts, with current applications such as databases.

Docker uses current kernel constructs such as cgroups and namespaces to run containers. This is why the Datadog agent employs the accounting metrics of the local cgroup to collect memory, I/O, network, and CPU metrics that are relevant to the containers. The process is done every 15 seconds like clockwork before the information is sent out to Datadog. This method is the simplest, but there is also a Dockerized version of the agent that is available for developers who want to use containers to run an entire piece of software.

In Datadog, developers define metrics using dashboards and graphs, which are based on tags. This technique allows a developer to track down the relative metrics for a lot of containers, and tags can then be utilized to create a graph.

# Component-level monitoring

End-to-end performance monitoring is very important for an application; it keeps tabs on the experience of the end-user, including whether the application or device works properly and how fast or slow it is. An end-to-end system consists of individual components, and so a component monitoring system keeps all individual components in check. For a mobile or web application, this includes the application server, the web server, the operating system, the physical and virtual machine, storage, and networking.

A component monitoring system detects and notifies applications and other components of a system that is either performing strangely or not performing at all. One excellent example of a product that does component-level monitoring is **Anturis**. Anturis works for in-house data centers and can also operate on the cloud. It detects anything out of the ordinary and alerts the web server by entering transactions similar to those of the user and testing the working and efficiency of the components that constitute any particular application. It measures disk I/O, CPU utilization, processes and threads, memory utilization, swap space, caching, storage, response time, and working efficiency.

Essentially, component-level monitoring is a thorough check of each component that makes up an application. It checks the performance of an application, keeps tabs on the working parts, detects abnormal behavior, checks the speed of components that make up an application, and ensures that the system runs smoothly.

The component-monitoring tool lets you dig down into your system's components and inspect issues that are related to performance. Sometimes, an external agent is required to keep tabs on the application's performance. So that the tool can decide what is normal, you need to enter cut-offs and set benchmarks in the application. When the response time surpasses set values, the dashboard raises red flags, but bear in mind that it's easier if limitations are set based on statistics and analysis rather than estimates. Monitoring is an important tool in application tuning; it could help, for example, to determine the storage space needed for data-hungry applications by monitoring their active hours.

# Domain-specific monitoring

While monitoring an environment for the occurrence of relevant events represents a key executive function, it's also necessary to be clear about which functions are mediated by domain-general or domain-specific mechanisms. Domain-specific monitoring offers you enough information that you can act rapidly if someone intrudes on your system. It acts like a scam detector by detecting activity in your name and keeping you posted. Domain name security covers all of the important features you'd expect, including things such as duplicate names, misspellings, and phonetic variations of your name.

Rather than relying on generic mechanisms to provide data monitoring, domain-specific monitoring introduces concept probes. These probes are in-sync with the business concepts that are used in the definition of business processes. They combine monitoring information from business process execution, service execution, and form aggregate information from a business perspective.

Domain-specific monitoring provides you with a better understanding of various business concepts parameters. It can also potentially help business process management and service-oriented architecture governance. This approach gives the technical user a thorough understanding of the contribution of each of the multiple application layers of the aggregate that makes up the combined performance of any particular business concept, which can help save time. Using domain-specific monitoring, your problems can be solved more quickly than usual, and you would get a faster response to changes in business partners, or any updates or improvements in the underlying infrastructure or application parameters.

Domain-specific monitoring caters to a large selection of businesses—not only to keep it guarded, but to merge concepts and create a new entity that helps users develop a faster response to the updates and changes software can develop over time. It determines the performance of a business concept and deals effectively with problems.

# Dashboards and identifying issues by going through logs

In a distributed application, we can use centralized logging, which provides a complete stack trace for a microservice-based application. To do this, you can use **Elasticsearch**, **Logstash**, and **Kibana** (**ELK**). In another of our books, *Mastering Spring Boot 2.0*, there is a complete practical example of how to implement centralized logging with ELK, and in this section we will provide you with an introduction to ELK. Take a look at the following diagram:

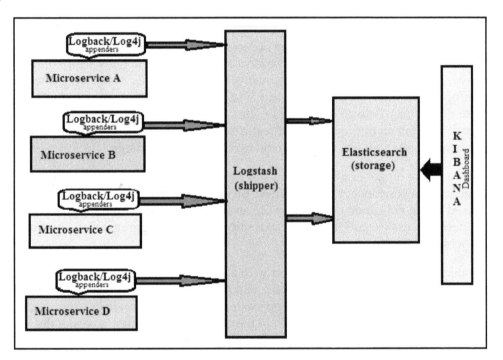

As you can see in the preceding diagram, we have successfully used **ELK.** The three open-source projects that make up ELK are as follows:

- **Elasticsearch**: Elasticsearch is an enterprise-grade search and analytics engine that can be widely distributed. It's an open-source search engine and is readily scalable. Elasticsearch can power extremely fast searches that support your data, provide analytical and statistic-based results, and support your data discovery applications.

- **Logstash**: Logstash is a server-side data processing pipeline that takes in data through multiple sources and, at the same time, powers it, converts it, and then sends it to a stash such as Elasticsearch. Logstash supports a variety of different forms of input and pulls in events from different sources simultaneously. It can take in information from your metrics, web applications, logs, data stores, and different AWS services, all of which stream without a hitch.

- **Kibana**: Kibana is a web interface that is used to search and view logs that Logstash has indexed. Kibana is also based on Elasticsearch. It's an open-source visualization platform that helps you visualize your data in a variety of charts, tables, and maps.

Take a look at the following screenshot, which shows the Kibana log dashboard:

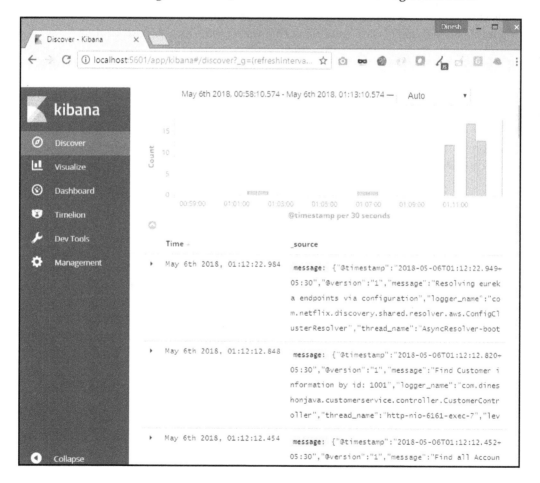

Whether you need to find the top $N$ outcomes in a sea of text-based documents, analyze security events, or take a closer look at your statistics, you've got a solution on the table with ELK.

# Grafana

Grafana, like Kibana, is commonly used in combination with Graphite, InfluxDB, Elasticsearch, and Logz.io. It is an open-source tool for visualization, and is used with data stores.

Grafana is essentially an advanced, faster, and more enriched version of the Graphite Web. It helps users with dashboard creation by providing a specific Graphite Target parser that provides smooth metrics and editing. Moreover, you can create smart axis format charts due to Grafana's fast, client-side rendering that uses Flotas as a default option.

Grafana is very easy to use, install, and set up. It supports installation on Linux, Mac, Windows, and Docker. Grafana is set up with an `.ini` file that is comparatively smoother to handle than Kibana's syntax-sensitive YAML setup files. Grafana even allows the use of environment variables to override the setup and configuration files. Grafana is built as a UI for the analysis of metrics, and it can multitask with different time-series data stores. Grafana comes with a unique query editor that is easily customizable to enable your data store's features and compatibilities.

# Summary

Monitoring the performance of a microservice-based application is very important. In microservice-based architectures, many services run separately to carry out a complete business task together, meaning we have to set up performance monitoring tools for each microservice. In this chapter, we discussed many different APM tools that act as an alternative. We also looked at various technologies that provide inter-service communication mechanisms, either synchronous or asynchronous, in a microservice-based application.

In this book, we have learned all about microservice architectures—from creating microservices to monitoring and testing.

# Other Books You May Enjoy

If you enjoyed this book, you may be interested in these other books by Packt:

**Hands-On Microservices with C#**
Matt R. Cole

ISBN: 9781789533682

- Explore different open source tools within the context of designing microservices
- Learn to provide insulation to exception-prone function calls
- Build common messages used between microservices for communication
- Learn to create a microservice using our base class and interface
- Design a quantitative financial machine microservice
- Learn to design a microservice that is capable of using Blockchain technology

**Hands-On Microservices with Node.js**
Diogo Resende

ISBN: 9781788620215

- Learn microservice concepts
- Explore different service architectures, such as Hydra and Seneca
- Understand how to use containers and the process of testing
- Use Docker and Swarm for continuous deployment and scaling
- Learn how to geographically spread your microservices
- Deploy a cloud-native microservice to an online provider
- Keep your microservice independent of online providers

# Leave a review - let other readers know what you think

Please share your thoughts on this book with others by leaving a review on the site that you bought it from. If you purchased the book from Amazon, please leave us an honest review on this book's Amazon page. This is vital so that other potential readers can see and use your unbiased opinion to make purchasing decisions, we can understand what our customers think about our products, and our authors can see your feedback on the title that they have worked with Packt to create. It will only take a few minutes of your time, but is valuable to other potential customers, our authors, and Packt. Thank you!

# Index

Roy Fielding 46

# S

server-side discovery pattern 67
serverless deployment 40
service communication
  approaches 44, 45
  asynchronous communication 52
  messaging 53
  synchronous communication 46
  transactional messaging 54
service deployment platforms 40
service discovery pattern
  about 65
  client-side discovery pattern 66, 67
  need for 64, 65
  server-side discovery pattern 67, 69
Service Registry
  about 69
  implementing, with Eureka 70
Service-oriented Architecture (SOA)
  about 16
  service consumer layer 17
  service provider layer 17
  versus microservice architecture 18
Simple Object Access Protocol (SOAP)
  about 19
  versus RESTful microservices 28
Spring Cloud's Netflix Zuul proxy
  used, for building API gateway 85, 87
synchronous communication, drawbacks
  strong coupling 46

  timeouts 46
synchronous communication
  about 46
  Apache Thrift 50, 51
  Google Remote Procedure Calls 48
  REST 46

# T

testing strategies
  about 90
  testing honeycomb strategy 91
  testing pyramid strategy 90
transactional messaging
  about 54, 55, 56
  benefits 55
  notification 55
  one-to-many service communication 56, 57
  one-to-one service communication 55, 56
  request/async response 55

# U

UI testing
  capture and replay 105
  manual-based testing 105
  model-based testing 105
unit testing
  about 92, 93
  code documentation 93
  example 93, 95
  test-driven development 93
  work check 93
unmarshalling 50

www.ingramcontent.com/pod-product-compliance
Lightning Source LLC
Chambersburg PA
CBHW080534060326
40690CB00022B/5125